Beyond Ego

THE *Mananam* SERIES

(*Mananam*–Sanskrit for "Reflection upon the Truth")

The Choice is Yours
Solitude
Vedanta in Action
The Mystery of Creation
Self-Discovery
Beyond Sorrow
On the Path
The Pursuit of Happiness
The Question of Freedom
Harmony and Beauty
The Razor's Edge
The Essential Teacher

(continued on inside back page)

Other Chinmaya Publication Series:

THE *Self-Discovery* SERIES

Meditation and Life
by Swami Chinmayananda

Self-Unfoldment
by Swami Chinmayananda

THE *Hindu Culture* SERIES

Hindu Culture: An Introduction
by Swami Tejomayananda

THE *Mananam* SERIES

Beyond Ego

CHINMAYA PUBLICATIONS

Chinmaya Publications
Chinmaya Mission West Publications Division
Main Office
P.O. Box 129
Piercy, CA 95587, USA

Chinmaya Publications
Chinmaya Mission West Publications Division
Distribution Office
560 Bridgetown Pike
Langhorne, PA 19053, USA
Phone: (215) 396-0390   Fax: (215) 396-9710
Toll Free: 1-888-CMW-READ (1-888-269-7323)

Central Chinmaya Mission Trust
Sandeepany Sadhanalaya
Saki Vihar Road
Mumbai, India 400 072

Credits:

Series Editors: Margaret Leuverink, Br. Rajeshwar
Editorial Assistants: Neena Dev, Neena Dewan, Nina Gandhi, Karen Gray,
          Rashmi & Arun Mehrotra, Mai Musta, Ann Poole, and Vinni Soni
Text Layout: David and Hazel Dukes
Cover design: Metro Label
Front Cover Photograph: Vijay Devan
Inside Illustrations: Neena Dev & Frank Richter

Library of Congress Catalog Card Number 98-93623

ISBN 1-880687-20-8

Contents

PART THREE

GOING BEYOND

Preface

The immortal teachers of the Upanishads had a most sublime outlook on life. These great masters were absorbed in a state transcending all concepts of "I" and "mine." And in order to convey this Truth to their students they "painted" beautiful poetic images, often using the sun as an analogy for the true Self.

Applying this imagery, let us imagine our true Self as a radiant sun, covered by a cluster of clouds. The clouds are our ego, the thoughts which prevent us from seeing the true Self within us. The clouds hide the sun so well that we cannot see it. Yet we know that they can never really cover the sun, they only appear to do so because of where we are standing. In the same way, our true Self is always present, but thought-clouds block our awareness of it. When thoughts are completely self-centered, the clouds are thick and dark. But as the clouds of egoism become less dense and more transparent, we begin to bask in the light of our true Self. We understand that it is our identification with our physical and mental equipment that has caused the illusion of ego. And the more we learn to identify with our higher Self the more the ego loses its grip on us. We realize that just as the heat of the sun dissolves the clouds; the fire of Knowledge burns the clouds of ignorance. This is the theme of "Beyond Ego," it shows us how to lift the cloud of ego so that we can enjoy a deeper and richer sense of being.

Wayne Dyer, author and lecturer, begins Part One "Understanding the Ego." He writes that freeing ourselves from the sense of ego becomes easier when we familiarize ourselves with its characteristics. Swami Chinmayananda, world-renowned teacher of Vedanta, points out that the ego is only a mistaken identity, and he explains how this mistaken notion has come about. Swami Prabhavananda of the Ramakrishna Mission uses two famous passages from the *Muṇḍaka Upaniṣad* to illustrate the difference between our apparent nature (the ego) and our real Nature.

In Part Two, "Letting Go," the authors show how we can become less identified with the ego through various spiritual practices. All these practices help purify the mind so that it can come to see the ego as merely a reflection of the true Self and not the absolute reality. Eknath Easwaran, teacher and founder of the Blue Mountain Center of Meditation, writes that fervent love of God is the only kind of love that is powerful enough to dissolve our ego. J. P. Vaswani, the Sindhi teacher, gives simple, practical suggestions to help break the hold of ego. The Buddhist writer and teacher, Sogyal Rinpoche, outlines three wisdom tools to help us unmask the ego and reawaken to our true nature. The contemporary American saint, Peace Pilgrim, outlines some of her steps to inner peace which helped her leave the self-centered life. In the letters of Swami Turiyananda, a direct disciple of Sri Ramakrishna, we see a teacher always ready to serve and guide his eager devotees. His essential message to his many correspondents always remained the same: Purify the mind, for when the ego (ignorance) ends, the self-luminous, ever present Self manifests itself.

When we are no longer living under the powerful influence of the ego, we begin to live from a higher plane and this becomes the topic of Part Three "Going Beyond." Swami Ramdas, whom his devotees lovingly called Papa, was the founder of Anandashram. He gives a unique remedy to help dissolve the subtle ego by the repetition of the Lord's name. Swami Jyotirmayananda, founder of Yoga Research Foundation, shows how Jesus' third beatitude from the Sermon on the Mount points to the majestic power of humility and meekness, and how these virtues are a natural outcome of the purified mind. Using verses from the *Bhagavad Gītā*, Swami Chinmayananda describes an egoless person and points out that the *Gītā's* plea to humanity is to become Soul-realized egos instead of ego-realized Souls. The Christian mystic, Jean Pierre de Caussade, writes that to abandon ourselves to the will of God is to sublimate our ego.

We end this book with Madan Mohan Varma's edited discourses of a saint who prefers to remain anonymous. He shows how deep yearning for God burns away all egoism and gives the devotee the capacity for complete surrender.

Thus we see that there is no relationship between the ego and our true Self, as the Self is real and the ego is a myth, only an idea that we have of ourselves. We are shown that all our conflicts are due to the idea of separateness, and that there is no sorrow for one who perceives the underlying unity in all. When the false self is no longer prominent the subtle voice of the true Self can be heard more and more. Reconnecting ourselves with the light of Self within, our hearts become still, without desire or judgment, and "the ego silently ends, just as the mist disappears at sunrise."

The Editors

PART ONE

Understanding the Ego

The blossom vanishes of itself as the fruit grows
So will your lower self vanish
As the Divine grows within.

Swami Vivekananda

A human being is part of a whole called by us the "Universe," a part limited in time and space. He experiences himself, his thoughts and feelings, as something separated from the rest—a kind of optical delusion of his consciousness. This delusion is a kind of prison for us, restricting us to our personal desires and to affection for a few persons nearest us. Our task must be to free ourselves from this prison by widening our circles of compassion to embrace all living creatures and the whole of nature in its beauty.

Albert Einstein
Dialogues with Scientists and Sages

From the Absolute standpoint everyone of us is, in our real Nature, eternally liberated, at all times. But the Spirit muffled by the covering of matter comes to gain for Itself the feeling of a separate ego existence. That ego, bound by its own projections through its own various equipments, feels that it is limited. Using the analogy of a bulb, we may say that the bulb is the equipment, and the electricity passing through the equipment manifests as light. Similarly, the life-force passing through the equipment of the mind and intellect manifests Itself as the ego. It is this mind that has come to misunderstand its own status and therefore, this mind, and its phantom-ego, needs the consolation and solace of liberation.

Swami Chinmayananda

I

Shattering the Illusion of Ego

by Wayne W. Dyer

The little three-letter word ego has had various meanings applied to it. In Freud's system, the ego is the conscious aspect of the psyche that chooses between the base instincts of the id and the morality of the superego. A person with an "ego-problem" is considered to be centered on the self. He is thought of as boastful, self-centered, and generally obnoxious. The stereotype is usually male and popularly referred to as being on an "ego trip."

There are many other interpretations of the word ego. Some view it as the unconscious part of ourselves, primarily involved with hate, malice, and destruction. Ego has also been described as something that is always with us, controlling our daily lives, but which we can do little to change. Others define ego as the exclusive physical aspect of our reality as opposed to the spiritual or higher part that we define as soul.

None of these are what I mean by ego. I look upon the ego as nothing more than an idea that each of us has about ourselves. That is, the ego is only an illusion, but a very influential one.

The Idea of Ego

No one has ever seen the face of ego. It is like a ghost that we accept as a controlling influence in our lives. The reason no one has seen the ego is because the ego is an idea.

The ego is a mental, invisible, formless, boundaryless idea. It is nothing more than the idea you have of your self—your body/mind/soul/self. Ego as a thing is nonexistent. It is an illusion. Entertaining that illusion can prevent you from knowing your true Self.

As I see it, ego is wrong-mindedness that attempts to present you as you would like to be rather than as you are. In essence, ego, the idea of yourself, is a backwards way of assessing and living life.

You have probably noticed the word *ambulance* written backwards on the front of a vehicle so that persons seeing it in their rearview mirror can read it. Think about it. When you look into a mirror, what you see is backwards. Your right hand is your left, your eyes are reversed. You understand that this is a backward view that you are seeing and you make the appropriate adjustments. You do not confuse reality with the image in the mirror.

The ego, this idea of yourself, is very much like the mirror example, *without* the adjustments. Your ego wants you to look for the inside on the outside. The outer illusion is the major preoccupation of the ego. The way of your higher Self is to reflect your inner reality rather than the outer illusion.

The description given by Sogyal Rinpoche in *The Tibetan Book of Living and Dying* is a wonderful explanation of this discovery: "Two people have been living in you all of your life. One is the ego, garrulous, demanding, hysterical, calculating; the other is the hidden spiritual being, whose still voice of wisdom you have only rarely heard or attended to." He then goes on to discuss what he calls your wise guide.

Inside of you there is a wise guide, a part of your true Self that walks with you as you progress along the path of your sacred quest. Rinpoche concludes: "The memory of your real nature, with all its splendor and confidence, begins to return to you. . . . You will find that you have uncovered in yourself your own wise guide. Because he or she knows you through and through, since he or she is you."

This inner wise guide is you, not the idea that you have of yourself. Think of this inner guide as your true Self and allow yourself to listen to this wise guide. Instead of listening to the gossip of the ego, you will hear clear and inspiring messages of wisdom. Eventually you will free yourself from the demands of the ego.

I am not suggesting that you conquer, defeat, or despise the ego. It is important to honor and love all aspects of ourselves. This includes the visible world of sensory perception and the invisible world of divine spirit.

This fourth and final key to higher awareness is about freeing yourself from the ego-sponsored illusion that the ultimate meaning and gratification of your life will be found outside of yourself. Taming the ego is a way of inviting the higher aspects of yourself to function in their natural, loving, and integrated design.

A Course in Miracles makes this point clear: "Your mission is very simple. You are asked to live so as to demonstrate that you are not an ego." If you are not feeling a deep, rich sense of yourself and your purpose in now-here, it is probably because you believe you are your ego.

Characteristics of Ego

Freeing yourself from the illusions of the ego will be easier when you recognize ego's characteristics.

1. Ego is your false self.

Your true Self is eternal. It is the God force within you that provides the energy for you to roam around in the clothes you call your body—a quiet, empty space surrounded by form. Believing you are only the physical self, the body enclosing the energy, is a false belief.

You need not repudiate the ego when you recognize it as a

false self. What you are really recognizing is the ego as an idea of the self that is inconsistent with your true, sacred identity.

We are more used to thinking we are a body with a soul than we are to realizing that we are a soul with a body. Viewing yourself in the way of the ego—with the emphasis on you as a physical being—is a form of amnesia, which is cured when you recognize who you truly are.

Tagore touches on the falsity of the ego in this telling passage:

> He whom I enclose with my name, is weeping in this dungeon. I am very busy building this wall all around; and as this wall goes up into the sky, day by day, I lose sight of my true being in its dark shadow. I take pride in this great wall, and I plaster it with dust and sand lest a least hole should be left in this name; and for all the care I take, I lose sight of my true being.

The wall is the ego that we construct. It imprisons us in a dungeon of frustration. Notice that Tagore uses "true being" to describe that which the ego shields from his awareness. The ego is the opposite of that true being. It is the false being—only an idea about the true being.

This idea has been with us ever since we began to think. It sends us false messages about our true essence. When we listen to it without the loving presence of the witness, we enter darkness. We make assumptions about what will make us happy and we end up frustrated. We push to promote our self-importance as we yearn for a deeper and richer life experience. We fall into the void of self-absorption repeatedly, not knowing that we need only shed the false idea of who we are.

2. Ego teaches separateness.

Ego wants to convince you to believe the illusion of separateness. With each painful experience of feeling alone, apart or separate, ego tightens its hold. This false belief is continually reinforced by our outer culture.

Convinced of our separateness, we view life as a competitive exercise. The competition increases the feeling of separateness and fosters anxiety about our place in the world. Unable to see ourselves connected to the invisible intelligence, the God force, our anxiety mounts and our sense of aloneness drives us to seek outer connectedness.

Substituting outer for inner connectedness is what you are attempting to do by needing to prove yourself better than others. Your need to look better, achieve more, accumulate more, judge others, and find fault are all symptoms of the erroneous belief that you are disconnected and separate.

The idea of separateness begins early in life. Without someone to model a rich inner life, we grow up experiencing the pain of loneliness, injuries, and peer criticisms, which intensify feelings of being apart from rather than a part of our true Self.

The ego's development is reinforced with the central belief in our separateness. We become convinced that the physical life is all that there is; we spend a lot of time believing we are better than others; our interpersonal philosophy is to get the best of the other guy first. Lack of purpose and meaning in life is countered with the belief that you are born, you shop, you suffer, and you die. Since this ego illusion is all there is to life, it becomes important to fight for what one wants and to defeat others.

The feelings of separation are so deep with this ego attitude that convincing someone otherwise is a major undertaking. However, you know inside yourself whether what you have just read describes you. And you can make the choice to no longer allow your ego to insist that you are separate from your sacredness.

When you drop ego beliefs, you are on the way to becoming one of those people Jean Houston describes who have managed to grasp their spiritual identity and fulfill their sacred quests. In a taped interview from New Dimensions Radio, Houston says of these people: "They all had little of narcissism, little of self-interest. They actually had very little self-consciousness at all. They simply didn't waste time worrying about their self-presentation. They were in love with life. They were in a state of constant engagement with all fields of life, whereas most people are encapsulated bags of skin, carrying around little egos." In order to get to this place you have to shatter the illusion of your separateness.

Your idea of yourself, which is what your ego is, will make itself known over and over as you attempt to shatter the illusion. And when you know that you are not separate, when that idea of yourself has shattered, you will experience a new kind of peacefulness.

No longer will you have to compete or be better than anyone. No longer will you need to accumulate, achieve, or seek outer honors. You will have left behind an idea that you had cultivated most of your life. Rather than view yourself as distinct from God and everyone else, you will experience your life as connected rather than separate.

The eternal aspect of your self will know its freedom to influence your life. You will experience the connectedness to your self and all life in a way that ego's illusion could not begin to comprehend.

3. Ego convinces you of your specialness.

The ego cannot recognize that the loving presence sees everyone as divine and lovable. "No one is special" is not an idea that the ego takes lightly. As a culture we tend to agree with ego that there are special people and special situations.

This attitude of specialness contributes to our social and economic problems by putting our country into debt and maintaining life support systems that mock the meaning of life.

Specialness implies that some are more worthy than others, as if God has favorites. When we offer this belief to our higher selves, we quickly see that it is preposterous. However, we allow our egos to create special categories and we ask others to honor them.

Specialness denies the perfect equality of creation. It also denies the totality of God's love. Your ego may insist that God loves you more than someone else, denying the totality of unconditional love that is God and that is you. Your ego's insistence also subjects you to the fear of not being special.

That fear of not being special then keeps you from knowing the peace of God, the harmony of oneness that leads to the bliss of your higher Self. Ego specialness prevents you from authentic feelings of your sacredness by creating an inner experience of fear. Self-esteem, which is a given because you are a spiritual being having a human experience, becomes dependent on believing you are special or virtuous in the eyes of God.

Who you are is not special. It is eternal, invisible, blissful, and sacred. Your self-esteem is not something you have to earn. A Self-realized person does not even think about self-esteem because he or she cannot doubt their value. They know to do so would be to doubt the value of God.

Attachment to your specialness creates enormous blocks to awakening to your true identity. It cultivates fear and resentment and prevents your awareness of unconditional love.

To discover your sacred Self is to let go of any attachment to specialness or identification with the ego. These are mere symbols of what you have come to regard as success. The ego encourages you to accumulate, believing you will increase your happiness. But you know that happiness is not found in the more-is-better lifestyle. You know that something outside of yourself cannot give you inner peace. You know that this is backwards thinking.

Turn those thoughts around. Look at the inner path, where you see yourself connected to God and all of life.

4. Ego is ready to be offended.

Whenever you are offended, you are at the mercy of your

ego. Setting up external rules of how you are to be treated is a way of guaranteeing a terminal state of being offended. It is the ego's way.

A favorite story of mine concerns Carlos Castaneda and his spiritual teacher, the Nagual don Juan Matus. After having been chased by a jaguar in the mountains for several days and being thoroughly convinced that this jaguar was going to tear him from limb to limb and eat him as his prey, Castaneda was finally able to escape the fierce beast.

For three days he had lived with the horrible fear that he was about to be shredded and devoured by the jaguar. When his teacher asks him about this experience, Castaneda, writing in *The Power of Silence*, replies:

> What had remained with me in my normal state of awareness was that a mountain lion—since I could not accept the idea of a jaguar—had chased us up a mountain, and that don Juan had asked me if I had felt offended by the big cat's onslaught. I had assured him that it was absurd that I could feel offended, and he had told me I should feel that same way about the onslaughts of my fellow men. I should protect myself, or get out of their way, but without feeling morally wronged.

All the things that offend you in some way play to your sense of self-absorption. That which offends you doesn't offend the real you, it offends your idea of who you are. In the world of the eternal you, nothing ever goes wrong, so there is nothing to be offended by.

But in the world of your ego, you are immediately jolted out of the blissful place of higher awareness into a world where you determine how others think, feel, and behave. When they are not the way you believe they should be, you are offended.

When you have sufficiently restrained your ego, you will be able to treat the onslaughts of others in the same way that Castaneda was taught to think about the jaguar. It obviously makes no sense to be "offended" by a jaguar's attack, because it is just doing what jaguars do.

Whether you like it or not, your fellow human beings are in some ways like the jaguar. They are doing what they do. If you can allow that without being offended, you will have put your ego's idea of who you are in its proper position in relation to the loving presence within you. Then you can be motivated to make the world a better place, without first needing to be offended.

When you have tamed your ego, you are no longer offended by your fellow humans. Free of ego's illusions, you see your fellow human beings as they are rather than as you think they should be. The way of your sacred Self becomes clearer.

5. Ego is cowardly.

Your ego thrives on convincing you that you are separate from God. To keep this belief strong, it promotes the illusion of your guilt and sinfulness in a cowardly attempt to avoid the face of God, which is your true Self.

The ego thrives on keeping you convinced that you are separate from God and will do anything to keep you in that mind-set. It will even take the coward's way of dealing with fear by encouraging your belief that you are a worthless sinner.

Your higher Self knows better. That loving presence knows that at the core of your being is a divine spirit, drenched in the light of love and bliss. When you find ideas of guilt continually surfacing, they are the cowardly acts of the ego, trembling in fear at the idea of your knowing that you are an extension of God.

But just as fear of the dark is transformed by turning on outer light, so is the cowardice of the ego transformed by your inner light. Cowardly behavior is simply a symptom of great fear. The antidote to fear is courage.

You can courageously deal with ego's fear and cowardice if you know that the part of God that you are is not separate from divine energy. That knowing provides the courage to shine the light of your inner love on the darkness of ego's fear. Thus illuminated, ego's idea—its illusion of you as exclusively a part of the physical world—is enlightened.

6. *Ego thrives on consumption.*

The false self will continually bombard you with the idea that you must have more in order to have peace. The ego pushes you toward external validation of yourself and is threatened by the notion that you can find peace within yourself. This push toward looking outward is what I have called "facing the wrong way."

The ego tries to keep you looking outward for your sense of peace and for a deeper and richer feeling of love. Its position would be weakened if you were to become acquainted with the love and richness within you. The ego is thus involved in a major endeavor to keep you facing the wrong way.

As you look outward in this futile attempt to find peace, you convince yourself that possessions will bring you the peace and fulfillment you yearn for. The ego has succeeded at this point in directing your life energy outward toward external pursuits, and it rejoices as you focus all your energy on acquisitions.

With your attention centered on what you see as wrong, you attempt to fix those wrongs by getting more of something outside of yourself. Those circumstances distract you from knowing the decision-making power of your mind to choose peace and love over anxiety and fear. This is how the ego system stays intact. It is imperative that you reclaim the power of your mind in order to transcend ego's false beliefs.

It is impossible to consume your way to peace. You cannot buy love. There is no peace in more-is-better, as I've already written. That way leads only to a lifetime of striving without ever arriving. The ego is threatened and frightened of your arriving. It wants you to consistently push yourself to new and more elaborate ways.

When you discontinue seeking what cannot be gotten from

outside of yourself, you arrive and relax in peacefulness. Your false self will be tamed.

7. *Ego is insane.*

My definition of an insane person is someone who believes that they are something they are not and acts on that belief in the world. This is precisely what the ego believes. And it is constantly attempting to convince you to believe that too.

The insanity persists because ego fears death. We could say that ego has an insane belief that it has to die if you start knowing your true Self. As this insanity takes hold of your life, you absolutely come to identify with this false idea of yourself. Unaware, you involuntarily join most of the rest of the world who also practice this insanity.

Keep in mind this quotation from *A Course in Miracles*: "This is an insane world, and do not underestimate the extent of its insanity. There is no area of your perception that it has not touched." Yet, the world is filled with people who are convinced that the holy spirit is something separate from them. And they spend their lives attempting to convince others of this insanity as well!

All human violence is a reflection of the belief in our separateness. If we knew we were all one and that God is within us, we would know that any harm to another is a violation of God. We would not be able to behave as we do to each other. But the insanity of the ego has convinced us that we are separate and encourages us to pursue our vendettas of hatred.

Pierre Teilhard de Chardin, the French theologian and paleontologist, wrote: "We are one, after all, you and I; together we suffer, together exist, and forever will recreate each other." This is sanity—knowing that you are one with God.

For the ego, this is a dangerous proposition to announce because it threatens ego's importance. Total capitulation to ego's fears is insanity. For instance, Teilhard de Chardin was forbidden by his Jesuit order to publish his metaphysical and philosophical papers. His pain must have been deeply felt, but his sanity was not compromised by an untamed ego. His knowing was stronger than ego and the church authorities. Today his published works are accepted classics.

One of the most insane ideas that your ego offers you is that you are morally and spiritually superior to those who are not consciously seeking their sacred selves. This idea of spiritual superiority is a separatist belief.

According to this belief, those who are spiritual are separate from those who are ego-bound. This is another ego trick attempting to satisfy your longing to know your higher Self, by creating a false dichotomy in which you are better than others. The reality is that there is no inherent superior/inferior dichotomy in humanness.

Each of us has our own path to traverse, and each of us will be tested in many ways. Your inner awareness of God does not make you superior to anyone—it simply brings you a deeper, richer sense of your purpose. Those who have not yet seen their inner light are still a part of you. They are you in other forms—different shapes with different behaviors.

The essence of you and of them is still the one Source; the celestial light of God. It is insane to let ego convince you to attach labels of inferior or superior to the loving presence within us all.

The above seven characteristics of the ego are merely an introduction to this topic. They are the primary general characteristics of how ego is involved in our individual lives.

You will experience a new kind of spiritual awakening as you become aware of ego's influence in your life. Real freedom is a result of freeing oneself from the power of the ego. However, ego will try to tempt you with many counterfeit freedoms along the path of your sacred quest.

II

Self-Discovery

by Swami Chinmayananda

Q: What is the significance behind the symbolism of the serpent in most religions?

A: The serpent that tempted Eve in the garden of Eden, the serpent upon which Lord Krishna danced and destroyed, the serpent that is worn as an ornament by Lord Shiva—all these represent the ego sense. This powerful, terrible serpent, (the ego) protects the treasure trove of blissful *Brahman*. This ego coils around the treasure and protects it for its own selfish ends. This ego (*ahamkāra*) does not allow us to realize the state of our blissful nature. It expresses itself at all times through some agitation or other.

The three hoods of the triple-hooded serpent are the *guṇa-s* (thought-quality or texture). The three types of *guṇa-s* are: *sattva* (pure), *rajas* (passionate), and *tamas* (dull). When the mind is in the *tāmasika* condition, it has to be whipped up with a dash of desire into the *rājasika* type. The *rājasika* mind must continue and even step up the dynamism of action, but give up more and more of its selfish attitudes. This selfless attitude lifts the mind into the peace and inner joy of the *sāttvika* type. With such a change in the texture of the mind, the personality of the individual also changes. It is only through the sword of Knowledge, gained through a sincere and intelligent study of the scriptures, and living up to its teachings that we can directly perceive the treasure of Bliss Absolute and thus end the ego. This is when we experience that the Self in us is the Self everywhere.

Q: How can we come to recognize this spiritual center in ourselves?

A: Ignorance of our true nature creates misunderstandings in us. This misunderstanding creates agitations of the mind and the negative thought veilings of the intellect which conceal the divine treasure within—the Self. When we identify ourselves with our ego we suffer. By developing a sense of "I'ness" and "myness" we see things around us that are not there, and are unable to see things that do exist. Thus we create a world of our own and suffer. Every spiritual practice is meant to help annihilate our false sense of ego. Once the false ego-conception has been broken down through discriminative analysis and deep meditation upon the truth of the Upanishadic declarations, we come to recognize the spiritual center in ourselves. Rediscovery of this center within ourselves is at once the experience of the total divine spiritual presence everywhere. Tasting a piece of sugar in any part of the world gives us the experience of all the sugar in the world, for all periods of time.

Thus the Upanishads declare that the Knower of *Brahman* becomes *Brahman*. As long as a drop of water is trembling at the tip of the finger, it is certainly separate from the ocean. The moment it falls into the ocean, however, it can no longer claim a separate name, form, or personality, but becomes one with the entire ocean. Similarly, as long as we identify ourselves with the delusive superimpositions, we will certainly have the dreamy experience of being separate. This is what we call the ego, and it has its own sense of limitation. As we become more aware of ourselves as pure Spirit, however, we gain the knowledge of its all-pervading nature, and become one with the supreme divinity.

Q: Could you please explain how our sense of ego comes about?

A: In the textbooks of Vedanta the ego is shown as part of the subtle body (*antaḥkaraṇa*). It is stated that the subtle body contains four functions: mind, intellect, ego, and *citta*. I will give a short explanation of each, but please keep in mind that these are merely functional designations of thought and not separate organs.

When a stimulus from the external world first enters us through the organs of perception, it causes a disturbance in thought. Thoughts in this condition of disturbance are called the mind. After the first impact is over, the disturbance dies down, and our thoughts come to a decision. Thoughts in this condition of decision are called the intellect.

A disturbance and a decision are related to each other only if they belong to a single individual. The awareness that both the disturbance and the decision belong to the individual is yet another thought, and its functional name is the ego. It is the feeling of "I'ness" and "my-ness."

Citta is the illuminating aspect in our thoughts that makes us aware of the other three functions. Through this function, we become aware of our mind and intellect and know that any thought we entertain is our own.

Pure Consciousness is unconditioned by any type of human equipment. However, when pure Consciousness functions through the mind, intellect, and the ego, it becomes as though conditioned by these types of equipment.

The ego exists in reference to the past. It is built upon memories of certain facts of life already experienced, such as "I am the daughter of so and so. I was educated at such and such a place. I loved, hated, won, lost and so on." In short, we are the sum total of all of our retained memories of our experiences in the past. That "I" concept also includes our hopes for the future. Since the ego is but a bundle of memories of the experiences lived by us in the past and the hope-filled thoughts about the future, it has no existence in the present moment. It thrives only in the burial-ground of the dead hours and in the womb of time. The ego is, in fact, a myth, a nonentity, a dream, a mere false shadow. All the sorrow and mortality belongs to this shadow of our own Reality. And in our thoughtlessness, we surrendered ourselves to the endless tyranny of this shadow lurking within us. "Detach yourself from this shadow. Know your real Self. Kill the tyrant within. It will bring the kingdom of perfection in your hearts." This is the clarion call of Vedanta. The scriptures only teach us the unreality of the nonexistent.

Q: How can the unreal veil the Real?

A: It is by a process of superimposition that the unreal has come to veil the Real. Superimposition is a mental trick, a juggling of our minds, by which it comes to misunderstand a thing to be something different from what it really is. The famous example is of the snake and the rope. In the darkness a person mistakes a rope for a snake and suffers from the false agonies of a "snakebite". Any amount of assurance that it is not a snake but only a rope, does not comfort the deluded sufferer. He will have to be led to the place and shown the rope. The moment he recognizes the rope, the "myth of the snake that bit him" disappears. The snake-idea rose up only in his mind. The snake born in his mind was removed when the knowledge of the rope dawned upon him. The snake appeared from ignorance of the rope, and when this ignorance is removed by knowledge, the snake, born of ignorance, is also removed.

Similarly, being ignorant of our own Reality, we have superimposed the ego upon ourselves. This superimposition ends with the knowledge of the Self. As the knowledge of the rope ended the agonies of the deluded victim, in the same way, the Knowledge of the Self ends the painful agonies of the ego (*jīva*). Our suffering does not depend upon the circumstances around us, but on the texture of our own mind. Our thoughts determine how we react to any given situation.

Past Impressions

Q: Why do we usually react instead of act?

A: Our actions are controlled by the mind, which in turn is controlled by the intellect. But the intellect decides and discriminates according to its past impressions. These are called *vāsanā-s* or *saṁskāra-s*. Every egocentric action performed in the past leaves an impression in our mind. The impressions or tendencies formed in our previous existence are stored in the unconscious, and they control our every thought and action.[1]

Ego is the needle that ruminates through the channels of thoughts which have become etched in the mind during earlier extroverted activities. If those lines are rightly made, perfect music of joyous peace can be ours. But if these channels are made of negative and animalistic thought-currents, the ego playing upon them can only sigh with fears and agitations. It is in this sense that the reaction of actions done in the past bind us in their relentless enslavement.

We could say that the sense of "I" or the ego is the mind and the intellect full of past impressions. But the intellect cannot act by itself. Consciousness vitalizes it and gives it the ability to react to the world. In the act of conscious thinking there are, as it were, two rays of consciousness, one doing the act of thinking and the other simply watching the process of thinking. But when there are many desires in the intellect, our thinking will be less clear and we become lost in our own imaginings. With fewer egocentric desires our thoughts decrease and we find it easier to watch the entire process of thinking.

Q: Can you elaborate on the role that the *vāsanā-s* play?

A: Every individual is born with a set of innate tendencies which are called *vāsanā-s*. They are a bundle of tendencies or desires which drive us to think, feel, and act in certain ways. Thus, it would be perfectly correct to say that we are what we are because of our *vāsanā-s*. The *vāsanā-s* create a desire in the intellect. The intellect passes it on to the mind where the desire causes agitations. Emotions and feelings then become so strong that the body is forced to carry out actions to satisfy these desires. The *vāsanā-s* are the iron curtain which act as an almost insurmountable barrier between each individual and God. Yet they are nothing but a bundle of egocentric desires. Once the *vāsanā-s* are removed, the ego itself will rediscover that it is nothing other than God.

Q: What is meant by egocentric desires?

A: Any desire which satisfies and pleases the ego or the "I" and "mine" sense in us.

Q: Since we seem to get some happiness through satisfying the egocentric desires, what is wrong in gratifying such desires?

A: First of all, there is no end to desires. As soon as one desire becomes satisfied another arises. When these desires cannot be satisfied, we become agitated and any agitation produces unhappiness. These agitations eventually cause loss of discrimination of the intellect and subsequently, remorse is experienced due to incorrect and impulsive thoughts and deeds.

The other important aspect of gratifying desires is that the satisfaction or happiness gained is fleeting. It is only temporary, while what we are actually seeking is a permanent happiness, peace of mind, and spiritual bliss. To obtain this, the body, mind, and intellect must be in harmony with the objects, emotions, and thoughts. Since both exist and function within the field of time, they are always changing, and, therefore, can never be in harmony for long. This leads to unhappiness and frustration.

Q: Then what are we to do? How can we achieve the goal of permanent, and unending happiness, peace, and bliss? What is it that prevents us from achieving that goal and how can we rid ourselves of that obstruction?

A: What really prevents us from achieving that goal are the *vāsanā-s*, which exert pressure on the mind and intellect. We must exhaust the *vāsanā-s* and turn our mind and intellect to the Higher in order to achieve this goal. It stands to reason that if the mind is agitated by desires, we are not happy. Desire is created or induced first in the intellect by the *vāsanā-s*. Therefore, if we exhaust our *vāsanā-s*, we end all egocentric desires, and our mind and intellect will be undisturbed and serene. Serenity, or an unagitated mind, confers happiness.

Q: How do we get rid of the *vāsanā-s*?

A: Let us recapitulate two important facts:

1) Egocentric "I" and "mine" types of desires gather or create more *vāsanā-s*. Selfless actions help decrease the *vāsanā-s*. With increasing egoless action, the *vāsanā-s* exhaust themselves.

2) A decrease in *vāsanā-s* means less pressure on the mind-intellect and thus fewer egocentric desires for the world of objects-emotions-thoughts.

Thus we see how *vāsanā-s* create actions, and from ego and desire-oriented actions more *vāsanā-s* are created. Since we have three main vehicles through which we function in the world, namely the body, mind, and intellect; we need to use them to exhaust our *vāsanā-s*. By creating healthy thoughts and performing right actions we ensure that we do not increase our *vāsanā-s*, but actually exhaust them.

Exhausting the *vāsanā-s* is the spiritual practice by which the ego rediscovers its own essential nature of freedom and peace. This unwinding of the *vāsanā-s* cannot be successfully undertaken merely through meditation at a fixed period of time during each day. Unless we are careful in our contacts with the world at every moment at our body, mind, and intellect levels, the unwinding cannot be completely successful.

Through meditation, no doubt, the subtle *vāsanā-s* are wiped out. But the grosser ones can be loosened and removed only in the fields of activity where we reaped these *vāsanā-s*. Hence *Niṣkāma Karma* [acting with detachment, without selfish, desire-prompted motives] is absolutely unavoidable. No other word in Hinduism is so badly misunderstood as *Niṣkāma Karma*. Detachment is easily misinterpreted as indifference. There is an ocean of difference between indifference and detachment. Indifference cannot bring forth the spiritual blossoming of an individual. Detachment from the world does not mean that we should not perceive forms, sounds, tastes, touches, or smells. As long as we have the five sense organs, the sense objects must have their effect on us. But it is the aftermath of this mental reception of the external stimuli that confuses us.

Lord Buddha was once insulted. He listened to the insult, and when the person finished, Lord Buddha quietly walked out. The disciple following him became angry, but the Lord's answer to the boy showed his great detachment. The Lord of Compassion said, "My boy, he gave me insults, but I did not receive them. Naturally these insults are with the very person who gave them to me. If you have received them you may return them; but I have not received them." It is not that Lord Buddha did not hear the sound of the words, but he did not bring his ego in to play upon these words.

Fancied imaginations spun by an uncontrolled mind at the impulses received from stimuli of the outer world are called *karmaphala* (consequences of action). To detach ourselves from these fruits of actions is the real detachment.

Character Development

Q: How important is character development in the process of annihilating the ego?

A: A person of character has least dissipation of thought. Human greatness is not muscular strength, but the greatness of character. Not only do the scriptures teach this, but this is also found to be true psychologically. A person is said to have character when he can influence his mind with his discriminative intellect even when the lower impulses rise in the mind. A good person is not one who never gets lusty thoughts, but one who has the strength to use the discriminative intellect to curb and redirect such thoughts in the right direction. As we build our character, our mental dissipations become less. A person without self-control, however, dissipates his mental powers. Whatever emotions rise in his mind, he has to act upon them. When we thus act from the emotions and the impulses of the moment, we have only the dignity of the animal and not the glory of the human being.

The difference between man and animal is that man has the capacity to discriminate and choose. When we do not use this faculty, we live impulsively. A person of character controls and regulates his impulses through his discriminative intellect. When our character is chastened, we discipline ourselves for a higher life. Moral stature is not only a strength for the individuals themselves, but it adds strength to the society or the community. Just think of the morally great Christ, or the Prince of Compassion, the Buddha. A great person's life is able to send out waves of influence, not just in their own life time, but as time passes, it gathers even new momentum. Therefore character building is absolutely necessary.

Self-love

Q: How does self-love differ from egoism?

A: Self-love is necessary—rather, unavoidable. As long as self-depreciation is a badge of humility and spirituality, we will find it difficult to reach the higher climbs of contemplation. To despise ourselves is to exhibit a gross lack of appreciation of our Source, the Lord. It is to accuse our creator of inadequacy and incompetence. How can an individual, who doubts his own love and goodness, ever be spiritual?

Another wrong perception of our self-love is that we equate what we are with what we have done. We ask ourselves: "How can I love myself when I have so many faults?" But we need not love our faults, nor love ourselves because of our successes and achievements. Despising our faults is different from blaming ourselves for having the faults. It is natural to make mistakes. Consider yourself as your own child. Children will be mischievous and will make mistakes. But parents will laugh them away.

Proper self-love is having faith in the goodness in ourselves. A sense of guilt only brings the same sin again and again into our mind. Don't just ask for forgiveness: forgive yourself. Holding onto guilt is still focusing on the ego. The Lord cannot forgive us as long as we are feeling guilty and bringing up the same idea again and again in our mind. If we accept and acknowledge the mistake, it is forgiven. Once surrendered to Him, forget and forgive yourself. It is so simple, if the surrender is total and complete.

Q: How do we go beyond the ego?

A: The way to go beyond ego (not kill it) is by selfless meditation, if this is not possible, total absorption in the task at hand, by living in the moment rather than for the moment.

Economic Problems

Q: How does the renunciation of the ego affect the world-situation? Does the understanding of *Ātman* solve any of the world's economic problems?

A: These are very interesting questions! Let us begin our investigation by asking: What are our economic problems? Inequity in the distribution of wealth, black-market profiteering, and exploitation of the poor by the rich. These are the main ones. We need not be great economists to know the cause for the inequity or the exploitation. Are these not the poisonous fumes of national and international sorrows, rising from the pool of selfishness and lust in individual hearts? And this selfishness and lust can again be traced back to our ego. Thinking ourselves to be separate individuals we frantically seek a permanent joy among the impermanent things of the world. And in this blind, mad rush each becomes pitted against another.

The moment one comes to experience the *Ātman*, the permanent, changeless Reality behind this seeming shadow-play called life, one has gone beyond all the so-called economic problems, which belong only to the waking-state world. Are the pain of hunger and thirst which you experienced in your dream still there when you are awake? Certainly not. Why? Because the "dreamer-I" was a false ego belonging only to the dream-state-consciousness. When passing into the waking-state-of-consciousness that dream-ego ends, and with that, the dream-famine has also ended.

In the same way, in God-consciousness, there is no waking-state-ego possible, and therefore, the waking-state-world and its economic problems are absent in the *Ātman*. One, who through spiritual practice and self-purification has cleansed himself and therefore dealt with the root of the problem, the ego, he alone can experience the *Ātman*. And if there be an intelligent generation which takes to the path of wise living, then in that generation there can be none of today's problems, such as inequity, lust, or exploitation. This is the ideal scheme of living we had in India many years ago, and it is also the plan we have for our village rehabilitation programs. It is the principle behind every revolutionary effort of humanity at reorganizing their generation. Unfortunately, in actual demonstration we find little effectiveness, for in working out our theories we often neglect to educate and insist that individuals live according to the standards of perfection, which are only attained through the renunciation of ego and the cultivation of universal love.

Your last question itself shows why every noble human attempt at constructive reorganization has met with expensive failures so far. You ask, "Does understanding of *Ātman*, and so on." A mere intellectual understanding of any noble ideal cannot help us, we must learn to live the ideal. Only then can its blessings be ours. Just as a mere understanding of peace will not end all war. Similarly, a mere understanding of *Ātman* will not solve our world's economic problems.

The Necessity of a Teacher

Q: Is a teacher necessary to help us progress on the spiritual path and attain the goal?

A: The very fact that you are asking this question clearly shows that we need teachers to teach us. Think for a moment: Is there anything that we do well today, or have any amount of mastery over, that has not been taught to us? If, for every perfect act in the world, in any activity, we need the guidance of an instructor, we can well understand the need for a teacher on the spiritual path, for here we have to deal with the subtlest of all forces, the mind and intellect. The teacher-disciple relationship is unavoidable. Every great master has been under the guidance of a teacher. It is not true to say that we can reach the goal just through books. A teacher is necessary. But we have to understand this relationship carefully. To say the teacher is necessary does not mean that all we have to do is meet the teacher and after that he will carry us to the goal.

The relationship between the teacher and the taught is exactly like that of the gardener and the flowers on the bush. The gardener does not create the flowers from the soil and the manure; the flowers come from the bush themselves. The gardener can only tend their roots, water, and protect them, and see that they have the right amount of sunlight and shade. He can only provide the externals. The gardener cannot guarantee the blossoming of the flower, that can only come from the bush itself.

In the same way, the teacher's job is to nurture the student with right thoughts. The student must be given a conducive and protective environment where he or she need not overstrain to live. But the blossoming into the real fragrance and beauty of the personality must come from within.

Thus, in the beginning of our spiritual quest a teacher is necessary, but as the student advances and the mind becomes quiet and concentrated, its subtler powers, called *siddhi-s*, come to manifest themselves. If we revel in the play of these psychic powers, we may never reach the goal. The teacher's help is necessary here also. He will ask, "Why are you lingering here? You may enjoy such fascinations in passing, but don't stay and play with these toys, for you are still only playing with the mind. Go forward."

Ultimately everyone will find exactly the teacher he or she needs for their present state of mental development. But understand that the only teacher is He, the Lord, who expresses in many forms.

The Realized Person

Q: How would you describe a person of perfection?

A: A person of perfection is one who has ended his ego and has come to rediscover his Self. When the needle has been taken off the record, even while the record is turning, not a single note, be it joyful or sorrowful, can be played. Similarly, whatever be the past actions and their consequent reactions registered upon the mind and intellect, unless that equipment is in contact with the false ego-needle it cannot act upon the individual. Thus it is said that a realized saint is beyond all reactions of karma. When a person has realized his true Self he becomes immortal. This immortality is never the status of the body. The body is made of matter and matter is finite. The state of immortality is a state which can be reached and experienced vividly, when ignorance has been removed. All spiritual practices are practices to help remove ignorance and bring liberation to the seekers.

Q: Is complete and total realization possible?

A: A dreamer upon waking no more doubts the nature and reality of the waking world. Similarly, an egocentric individual, upon realizing God-Consciousness, is so consumed with that realization that there is no doubt left in him as to the reality of this present experience. Beyond all darkness, this inner experience is extremely clear and supremely subjective. There is no doubt in the individual regarding the nature and reality of this experience. Complete and total realization is possible. This is the assertion of all Vedantic Seers.

FOOTNOTE:

[1] Yoga-psychology agrees with Freud that the conscious is controlled
and guided by the unconscious, but it insists that there is a power
inherent in the mind, which can overcome the unconscious and all
its tendencies, and where complete transformation of character may
be achieved in the end.

III

Our Sense of Ego

By Swami Prabhavananda

I will begin by quoting two famous passages from the *Muṇḍaka Upaniṣad*: "Like two birds of beautiful golden plumage—inseparable companions—the individual self and the immortal *Ātman* are perched on the branches of the selfsame tree. The former tastes the sweet and bitter fruits of the tree. The latter remains motionless, calmly watching."

"The individual self, deluded by forgetfulness of its identity with the *Ātman*, grieves, bewildered by its own helplessness. When it recognizes the Lord—who alone is worthy of our worship—as its own *Ātman*, and beholds its own glory, it becomes free from all grief."

These are revealed truths. They have been directly and immediately experienced by the seers and sages, within the depths of their own souls. Such truths are, of course, universal, and can be realized by every one of us who is ready to make the effort to do so.

The fable of the two birds is intended to teach us the truth about man's real and apparent nature. It teaches that man suffers only because he is ignorant of his true Being. God is. He is the absolute Reality, "ever-present in the hearts of all." He is the blissful *Ātman* which sits calmly watching the restlessness of its companion. And the fable goes on to tell us that, at last, the two birds merge into one. The *Ātman* is all that exists.

Therefore, our suffering has no real cause, no necessity.

This external life, this tasting of the sweet and bitter fruits of the tree of experience, is a dream from which, at any moment, we may awake. Sometimes our dream is pleasant, sometimes unpleasant. There are philosophers who tell us that the unpleasant and evil things of life are an illusion, and that only the pleasant and good things are real. But this cannot be true. Pleasure and pain, good and evil, belong inseparably together—they are what Vedanta calls "the pairs of opposites." They are like the two sides of a coin. Their nature cannot differ. Either both are real or both are unreal.

Theologians have argued for centuries over the problem of evil. Why is man unaware of his divine Nature? But this question could only be answered by those who have transcended our human consciousness, with its belief in good and evil. Why do we dream? We can only find the answer to that problem after we have awakened. The seers who have attained transcendental consciousness tell us that the so-called problem of evil is no problem at all, because evil does not exist and has never existed. But for us who still live in the consciousness of the relative world, the problem of how our ignorance arose is merely academic. We need only ask how we shall remove our ignorance.

What is the nature of this ignorance? It resides in our sense of ego, our belief that we are individual beings. The ego veils our eyes, as it were, and causes us to dwell in ignorance. Man is the *Ātman*, the Spirit. He has a mind, senses, and a body. When he forgets that he is the *Ātman*, and identifies himself with body, mind, and senses, then the sense of ego originates. With the birth of this ego-sense, the transcendental nature is forgotten. Man lives on the sense plane and becomes subject to the law of karma and rebirth.

In our ignorance, we are no longer aware of the Lord within us, and yet, because our true nature is divine, we feel a lack, an emptiness. We want to find something, although we do not know exactly what it is. We want some kind of happiness which will be lasting. And so desire rises in us, a craving for everything which seems to promise happiness and seems pleasant, and a shrinking back from everything which seems unpleasant. Behind all our desires—even the very lowest and basest—there is the urge to find real, unalloyed happiness and freedom, to find immortality. This strong craving, which does not know what is its real objective, involves us in all sorts of action. We try everything, in order to find what it is that we are seeking. And our actions, in their turn, involve us in the limitations and bondage of karma; as we sow, so we reap. We begin to taste the fruits of the tree of experience. We wish to taste only the sweet fruits, but this is impossible, for the bitter fruit grows on the same tree, and we cannot have the one without the other.

Separation from our True Nature

Out of this attachment to what is pleasant and this aversion to what is unpleasant, there grows a clinging to life. The ego clings to its sense of individuality; it does not want to die. Yet this "life" to which the ego clings is really death, because it is separation from our true nature, from God. That is why Jesus said: "For he who would save his life will lose it; but he who loses his life for My sake will find it." (*Matthew, Chapter 16:25.*)

To find real life, the life of our true nature, we must transcend the ego. We shall never know happiness until we realize *Brahman*, the Ground in which we are rooted. The ego is the only barrier to this knowledge. Sri Ramakrishna used to say that when the ego dies, all troubles cease. And Jesus tells us: "Except a man be born again, he cannot enter the Kingdom of God." This rebirth, this birth in spirit, is the death of the ego. The Hindus have a saying: "Die while living." Die to the ego and be reborn spiritually, even in this life.

So the problem of all spiritual life, no matter whether you are a Christian, Buddhist, or a Hindu simply amounts to this: How can I kill the ego? And the answer given by every one of these religions is the same: Surrender yourself. Give yourself up to God, completely and wholeheartedly. Love God with all your heart, all your soul, and all your mind. Become absorbed, and forget yourself in the consciousness of God. The ego is the only obstacle to God-consciousness. The great yogi, Patanjali, compares it to the bank of a reservoir. In the reservoir there is plenty of water—the living water of *Ātman*. If we want to irrigate our fields, all we have to do is to break down the bank, and water will flow over the fields. Each one of us has that reservoir inside him, ready to flood his life with joy, wisdom, and immortality if only he will break down the ego, the barrier.

The Practice of Discrimination

It sounds so simple: to love God, to surrender ourselves to Him, to kill this ego. But it is the hardest thing one can possibly do. It involves great spiritual disciplines; and the practice of these disciplines with the utmost patience and perseverance. The mind is always straining to go outward, towards everything that seems pleasant in the external world. And the ego reasserts itself perpetually. In whatever way we may try to banish it, it keeps reappearing, as it were, in different disguises. So we have to keep on trying.

What are these disciplines we have to practice? They are discrimination (*viveka*) and dispassion (*vairāgya*). We have to discriminate, perpetually, throughout our lives, between what is real and what is unreal. God, the infinite, the unchanging, is the only reality. Everything else, all appearances and forms of the external world, are unreal. As you practice this discrimination, you become convinced that God is, that He really exists. And, furthermore, you begin to realize that if there is a God, He must be attainable.

Most people think that they believe in God, and there it ends. They imagine that mere belief in God is enough. It is sufficient to be what they call "a God-fearing man." But the great spiritual teachers have told us that religion means something far more than mere faith, a mere opinion that God exists. You have to believe that God is actually attainable. Otherwise, the practice of dispassion and discrimination does not mean anything at all. Simply by saying that we believe in God we cannot free ourselves from these experiences of life and death, pleasure and pain. These are the direct, immediate experiences of the dream which we call life. We have to wake up from this dream, and know the Reality, which is also a direct, immediate experience. We have to break this dream while living on earth. We have to die while living, in order to enter the Kingdom of God. The proof of God's existence is not to be found in theological arguments, or even in the revealed scriptures. Yes, Jesus saw God, Ramakrishna saw God, but that is no proof for us. We must see God for ourselves, that is the only real proof.

Again, the practice of dispassion and discrimination does not mean that we are to give up the activities of life. It does not mean running away from the world. It is the mind which has to be trained. We have to cultivate yearning for God. We have to train our minds in such a way that we are surrendering our ego to God, every moment of our life.

Yearning for God

How shall we cultivate this yearning, this love for God? It cannot be done simply by sitting down, closing our eyes and fixing our hearts on God. That is only possible at a very advanced stage. What shall be our method of training? The *Gītā* teaches *karma yoga*. In *karma yoga* we learn to surrender ourselves to God through our actions, through every breath we breathe. There are different ways of doing this. For instance, you can regard yourself simply as a machine. Who is the operator? The *Ātman* within you. You have to try to forget the ego: for a machine has no will of its own. Or you can think of the fable of the two birds. You are the *Ātman*, motionless, actionless, calmly observing. The senses move among the sense objects, but you remain free from all action. You are actionless in the midst of action. Or again you can make every action into a sort of ritual, an offering to God. As Lord Krishna says to Arjuna, in the *Gītā*:

> Whatever your action,
> Food or worship,
> Whatever the gift
> That you give to another,
> Whatever you vow
> To the work of the Spirit,
> Oh! son of Kunti,
> Lay these also
> As offerings before Me.[1]

And He continues, "Thus you will free yourself from both the good and the evil effects of your actions. Offer up everything to Me. If your heart is united with Me, you will be set free from karma even in this life, and come to Me at last."

When you fall in love with someone, your mind dwells on that person, no matter what you may be doing all day long. That is how we should love God. Every day, we must fall in love with Him afresh, in a new way. Human love wears out and ceases, but love of God grows. You do not get tired of it. It is always a new thing. It gains in intensity. To cultivate this love, we must try to be conscious of God continually; and this is only possible if we practice regular meditation. Without meditation, *karma yoga* is impracticable. Just by being a good person, by living an ethical life, by trying to be selfless in your service, you cannot reach the transcendental Reality. By meditation, you have to awaken the power that is within you. Then you begin to see the play of God in the outside world. Ethical life and service are an aid, but they are not an end in themselves. The end is to be one with God. Set aside some time each day to devote yourself completely and wholeheartedly to the contemplation of God. Think of nothing else but Him, and so the practice will become easy.

Where should we think of God? We are not to pray to some external Being who hangs in the sky. God is omnipresent. He is nearer than anything we know. He is within us. We have to feel that living Presence within the chamber of our own hearts. Go into your own heart and surrender yourself there, to the Ruler of the universe, without whom you could not breathe or act, without whom there is no consciousness, no reality. Surrender yourself completely and wholeheartedly to Him.

FOOTNOTE:

[1] *Bhagavad-Gītā*, 9:27.

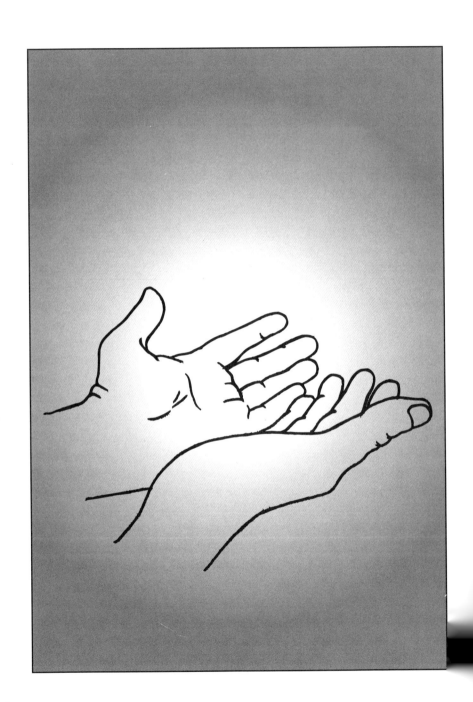

PART TWO

Letting Go

*When did the flute have to worry about the
audience
Or judge what to play next?
Be a flute in His hands.
Only when you are acting with ego can you
get exhausted physically,
upset emotionally, and confused
intellectually.*

Swami Chinmayananda

To a painter the teacher said: "To be successful every painter must invest hours in unremitting toil and effort. To some it will be given to let go of the ego as they paint. When this happens, a masterpiece is born." Later a disciple asked, "Who is a Master?" The teacher replied, "Anyone to whom it is given to let go of the ego. Such a person's life is then a masterpiece."

Anthony de Mello

The only thing which a person must renounce if he wishes to attain the Supreme Truth is the notion of individuality—nothing else. A person who is entirely free from the ego-sense is the happiest person in the world. Because he has found God—absolute Existence, Consciousness, and Bliss—in place of the ego.

Swami Ramdas

IV

The Wisdom of Egolessness

by Sogyal Rinpoche

I sometimes wonder what a person from a little village in Tibet would feel if you suddenly brought him to a modern city with all its sophisticated technology. He would probably think he had already died and was in the bardo[1] state. He would gape incredulously at the planes flying in the sky above him, or at someone talking on the telephone to another person on the other side of the world. He would assume he was witnessing miracles. And yet all this seems normal to someone living in the modern world with a Western education, which explains the scientific background to these things, step by step.

In just the same way, in Tibetan Buddhism there is a basic, normal, elementary spiritual education, a complete spiritual training for the natural bardo of this life, which gives you the essential vocabulary, the ABC's of the mind. The bases of this training are what are called the "three wisdom tools," the wisdom of listening and hearing; the wisdom of contemplation and reflection, and the wisdom of meditation. Through them we are brought to reawaken to our true nature, through them we uncover and come to embody the joy and freedom of what we truly are, what we call "the wisdom of egolessness."

Imagine a person who suddenly wakes up in hospital after

a road accident to find she is suffering from total amnesia. Outwardly, everything is intact: she has the same face and form, her senses and her mind are there, but she doesn't have any idea or any trace of a memory of who she really is. In exactly the same way, we cannot remember our true identity, our original nature. Frantically, and in real dread, we cast around and improvise another identity, one we clutch onto with all the desperation of someone falling continuously into an abyss. This false and ignorantly assumed identity is "ego."

So ego, then, is the absence of true knowledge of who we really are, together with its result: a doomed clutching on, at all costs, to a cobbled together and makeshift image of ourselves, an inevitably chameleon charlatan self that keeps changing and has to, to keep alive the fiction of its existence. In Tibetan, ego is called *dak dzin*, which means "grasping to a self." Ego is then defined as incessant movements of grasping at a delusory notion of "I" and "mine," self and other, and all the concepts, ideas, desires, and activity that will sustain that false construction. Such a grasping is futile from the start and condemned to frustration, for there is no basis or truth in it, and what we are grasping at is, by its very nature, ungraspable. The fact that we need to grasp at all and go on and on grasping shows that in the depths of our being we know that the self does not inherently exist. From this secret, unnerving knowledge spring all our fundamental insecurities and fear.

As long as we haven't unmasked the ego, it continues to hoodwink us, like a sleazy politician endlessly parading bogus promises, or a lawyer constantly inventing ingenious lies and defenses, or a talk show host going on and on talking, keeping up a stream of suave and emptily convincing chatter, which actually says nothing at all.

Lifetimes of ignorance have brought us to identify the whole of our being with ego. Its greatest triumph is to inveigle us into believing its best interests are our best interests, and even into identifying our very survival with its own. This is a savage irony, considering that ego and its grasping are at the root of all our suffering. Yet ego is so convincing and we have been its dupe for so long, that the thought that we might ever become egoless terrifies us. To be egoless, ego whispers to us, is to lose all the rich romance of being human, to be reduced to a colorless robot or a brain-dead vegetable.

Ego plays brilliantly on our fundamental fear of losing control and of the unknown. We might say to ourselves: "I should really let go of ego, I'm in such pain, but if I do, what's going to happen to me?"

Ego will chime in, sweetly: "I know I'm sometimes a nuisance and believe me, I quite understand if you want me to leave. But is that really what you want? Think: If I do go, what's going to happen to you? Who will look after you? Who will protect and care for you like I've done all these years?"

And even if we were to see through ego's lies, we are just too scared to abandon it; for without any true knowledge of the nature of our mind, or true identity, we simply have no other alternative. Again and again we cave in to its demands with the same sad self-hatred as the alcoholic feels reaching for the drink that he knows is destroying him, or the drug addict groping for the drug that she knows will only leave her flat and desperate after a brief high.

Ending the Tyranny

To end the bizarre tyranny of ego is why we go on the spiritual path, but the resourcefulness of ego is almost infinite and it can at every stage, sabotage and pervert our desire to be free of it. The truth is simple, and the teachings are extremely clear; but I have seen again and again, with great sadness, that as soon as they begin to touch and move us, ego tries to complicate them because it knows it is fundamentally threatened.

At the beginning, when we first become fascinated by the spiritual path and all its possibilities, ego may even encourage us and say: "This is really wonderful. Just the thing for you! This teaching makes total sense!"

Then when we say we want to try meditation practice, or go on a retreat, ego will croon: "What a marvelous idea! Why don't I come with you. We can both learn something." All through the honeymoon period of our spiritual development, ego will keep urging us on: "This is wonderful—it's so amazing, so inspiring . . ."

But as soon as we enter what I call the "kitchen sink" period of the spiritual path, and the teachings begin to touch us deeply, unavoidably we are faced with the truth of ourselves. As the ego is revealed, its sore spots are touched, and all sorts of problems start arising. It's as if a mirror we cannot look away from were stuck in front of us. The mirror is totally clear but there is an ugly, glowering face in it, our own, staring back at us. We begin to rebel because we hate what we see. We may strike out in anger and smash the mirror, but it will only shatter into hundreds of identical ugly faces, all still staring at us.

Now is the time we begin to rage and complain bitterly; and where is our ego? Standing staunchly by our side, egging us on: "You're quite right, this is outrageous and unbearable. Don't stand for it!" As we listen enthralled, ego goes on to conjure up all sorts of doubts and demented emotions, throwing fuel on the fire: "Can't you see now this is not the right teaching for you? I told you so all along! Can't you see he is not your teacher? After all, you are an intelligent, modern, sophisticated, Western person, and exotic things like Zen, Sufism, meditation, Tibetan Buddhism belong to foreign, Eastern cultures. What possible use could a philosophy made up in the Himalayas, a thousand years ago be to you?"

As ego watches us gleefully become more and more ensnared in its web, it will even blame all the pain, loneliness, and difficulties we are going through as we come to know ourselves on the teaching, and even on the teacher: "These gurus don't care anyway, whatever you're going through. They are only out to exploit you. They just use words like 'compassion' and 'devotion' to get you in their power . . ."

Ego is so clever that it can twist the teachings for its own purposes, after all, "The devil can quote scriptures for his own ends." Ego's ultimate weapon is to point its finger hypocritically at the teacher and his followers, and say: "No one around here seems to be living up to the truth of the teachings!" Now ego poses as the righteous arbiter of all conduct: the shrewdest position of all from which to undermine your faith, and erode whatever devotion and commitment to spiritual change you have.

Yet, however hard ego may try to sabotage the spiritual path, if you really continue on it, and work deeply with the practice of meditation, you will begin slowly to realize just how gulled you have been by ego's promises: false hopes and false fears. Slowly you begin to understand that both hope and fear are enemies of your peace of mind, hopes deceive you, and leave you empty and disappointed, and fears paralyze you in the narrow cell of your false identity. You begin to see also just how all-encompassing the sway of ego has been over your mind, and in the space of freedom opened up by meditation, when you are momentarily released from grasping, you glimpse the exhilarating spaciousness of your true nature. You realize that for years, your ego, like a crazy con artist, has been swindling you with schemes and plans and promises that have never been real and have only brought you to inner bankruptcy. When, in the equanimity of meditation, you see this, without any consolation or desire to cover up what you've discovered, all the plans and schemes reveal themselves as hollow and start to crumble.

This is not a purely destructive process. For alongside an extremely precise and sometimes painful realization of the fraudulence and virtual criminality of your ego, and everyone else's, grows a sense of inner expansiveness, a direct knowledge of the "egolessness" and interdependence of all things, and that vivid and generous humor that is the hallmark of freedom.

Because you have learned through discipline to simplify your life, and so reduced the opportunities for ego to seduce you, and because you have practiced the mindfulness of meditation, and, through it, loosened the hold of aggression, clinging, and negativity on your whole being, the wisdom of insight can slowly dawn. And in the all-revealing clarity of its sunlight this insight can show you, distinctly and directly, both the subtlest workings of your own mind and the nature of reality.

The Wise Guide

Two people have been living in you all your life. One is the ego, garrulous, demanding, hysterical, calculating; the other is the hidden spiritual being, whose still voice of wisdom you have only rarely heard or attended to. As you listen more and more to the teachings, contemplate them, and integrate them into your life, your inner voice, your innate wisdom of discernment, what we call in Buddhism "discriminating awareness," is awakened and strengthened, and you start to distinguish between its guidance and the various clamorous and enthralling voices of ego. The memory of your real nature, with all its splendor and confidence, begins to return to you.

You will find, in fact, that you have uncovered in yourself your own wise guide. Because he or she knows you through and through, since he or she is you, your guide can help you, with increasing clarity and humor, negotiate all the difficulties of your thoughts and emotions. Your guide can also be a continual, joyful, tender, sometimes teasing presence, who knows always what is best for you and will help you find more and more ways out of your obsession with your habitual responses and confused emotions. As the voice of your discriminating awareness grows stronger and clearer, you will start to distinguish between its truth and the various deceptions of the ego, and you will be able to listen to it with discernment and confidence.

The more often you listen to this wise guide, the more

easily you will be able to change your negative moods yourself, see through them, and even laugh at them for the absurd dramas and ridiculous illusions that they are. Gradually you will find yourself able to free yourself more and more quickly from the dark emotions that have ruled your life, and this ability to do so is the greatest miracle of all. Terton Sogyal, the Tibetan mystic, said that he was not really impressed by someone who could turn the floor into the ceiling or fire into water. A real miracle, he said, was if someone could liberate just one negative emotion.

More and more, then, instead of the harsh and fragmented gossip that ego has been talking to you all your life, you will find yourself hearing in your mind the clear directions of the teachings, which inspire, admonish, guide, and direct you at every turn. The more you listen, the more guidance you will receive. If you follow the voice of your wise guide, the voice of your discriminating awareness, and let ego fall silent, you come to experience that presence of wisdom and joy and bliss that you really are. A new life, utterly different from that when you were masquerading as your ego, begins in you. And when death comes, you will have learned already in life how to control those emotions and thoughts that in the states of death, the bardos, would otherwise take on an overwhelming reality.

When your amnesia over your identity begins to be cured, you will realize finally that *dak dzin*, grasping at self, is the root cause of all your suffering. You will understand at last how much harm it has done both to yourself and to others, and you will realize that both the noblest and the wisest thing to do is to cherish others instead of cherishing yourself. This will bring healing to your heart, healing to your mind, and healing to your spirit.

It is important to remember always that the principle of egolessness does not mean that there was an ego in the first place, and the Buddhists did away with it. On the contrary, it means there was never any ego at all to begin with. To realize that, is called "egolessness."

The Three Wisdom Tools

The way to discover the freedom of the wisdom of egoless-ness, the masters advise us, is through the process of listening and hearing, contemplation and reflection, and meditation. They advise us to begin by listening repeatedly to the spiritual teachings. As we listen, they will keep on and on reminding us of our hidden wisdom nature. It is as if we were that person I asked you to imagine, lying in the hospital bed suffering from amnesia, and someone who loved and cared for us were whispering our real name in our ear, and showing us photos of our family and old friends, trying to bring back our knowledge of our lost identity. Gradually, as we listen to the teachings, certain passages and insights in them will strike a strange chord in us, memories of our true nature will start to trickle back, and a deep feeling of something homely and uncannily familiar will slowly awaken.

Listening is a far more difficult process than most people imagine; really to listen in the way that is meant by the masters is to let go utterly of ourselves, to let go of all the information, all the concepts, all the ideas, and all the prejudices that our heads are stuffed with. If you really listen to the teachings, those concepts that are our real hindrance, the one thing that stands between us and our true nature, can slowly and steadily be washed away.

In trying really to listen, I have often been inspired by the Zen master Suzuki-roshi, who said: "If your mind is empty, it is always ready for anything; it is open to everything. In the beginner's mind there are many possibilities, in the expert's mind there are few."[2] The beginner's mind is an open mind, an empty mind, a ready mind, and if we really listen with a beginner's mind, we might really begin to hear. For if we listen with a silent mind, as free as possible from the clamor of preconceived ideas, a possibility will be created for the truth of the teachings to pierce us, and for the meaning of life and death to become increasingly and startlingly clear. My master Dilgo Khyentse Rinpoche said: "The more and more you listen, the more and more you hear; the more and more you hear, the deeper and deeper your understanding becomes."

The deepening of understanding, then, comes through contemplation and reflection, the second tool of wisdom. As we contemplate what we've heard, it gradually begins to permeate our mind stream and saturate the inner experience of our lives. Everyday events start to mirror and more and more subtly and directly to confirm the truths of the teachings, as contemplation slowly unfolds and enriches what we have begun to understand intellectually and carries that understanding down from our head into our heart.

The third tool of wisdom is meditation. After listening to the teachings and reflecting on them, we put into action the insights we have gained and apply them directly, through the process of meditation, to the needs of everyday life.

FOOTNOTE:

[1] The word "bardo" is commonly used to denote the intermediate state between death and rebirth.

[2] Shunryu Suzuki, *Zen Mind, Beginner's Mind,* 21.

V

Dethroning the Ego

by J.P. Vaswani

Away from the city's roar and ignoble strife, I sat in a silent corner in the garden. The flowers smiled. Little raindrops pattered on the new leaves of summer. But my heart was not happy.

"So many books have I read," I soliloquized. "So many lives of saints have I studied. And every morning as I wake up, I recite from the scriptures. And every evening I attend the satsang (fellowship meeting) with clock-like punctuality. But, alas! year after year hath passed away and I am no nearer the Goal. I see no improvement in myself. And I often wonder if I am progressing or regressing."

In utter dejection, I wept tears of sorrow. I came to Sadhu Vaswani and opened out my heart's grief at his feet. In a voice, at once sweet and tender, he said: "Weep not, my child! But listen to what I say!"

There was something in his words which made me forget my sorrow. The clouds were lifted; and the sun shone again!

"Speak that your servant may listen," I said.

And Sadhu Vaswani said, "It is true you have read many books. But to the Pilgrim on the Path books are a burden. You say you have studied the lives of saints, but your daily life does not bear witness to it. To study is not to turn over the pages of a book. To study is to ponder well, to meditate, and to assimilate the teaching in one's life. Every morning you read from the scriptures, but are you any better than the parrot who keeps on reciting the name of God? And every evening you go to the satsang at the right time, but are you any better than the temple-bell which, at the exact hour, calls the worshipers to the shrine?"

The words were true, too true. I felt humbled. And I said, "Now I understand why I have wasted my years in vain. Tell me what I need to do."

And Sadhu Vaswani said, "Many are the things I would tell you. But not all at once. Gradually I shall unfold to you the pattern of life which you may follow to develop your spiritual powers. Let me pass on to you the first lesson for today."

"What is it?" I eagerly asked.

And Sadhu Vaswani said, "Remember, the one barrier between you and God is the ego. And, instead of putting it down, you strengthen it and hug it to yourself as your dearest friend. Your actions, thoughts, and flights of imagination only feed the ego, until it has become your master and lord. Break the tyranny of the ego, this is my first word to you!"

Practical Instructions

And I said, "I understand what you have spoken. I pray that you give me some simple practical instructions which I may follow in my daily life to displace the ego from its position of sovereignty and unlimited power."

And Sadhu Vaswani said, "A few simple suggestions let me give to you today."

(1) When in the midst of friends or strangers, refrain from pushing yourself forward. See how at the slightest excuse you try to show yourself off!

(2) Refrain from much talk. The less you talk, the less you will be noticed and the more you will be permitted to recede in the background. As it is, you talk too much, and always try to monopolize conversation. Only this morning, a friend came to you

and tried to speak to you of the burden on his mind. He had scarcely begun when you cut him short and delivered to him a discourse on accepting the Will of God. Can you truthfully say that in every situation of life you accept the Will of God? Then what right do you have to lecture to others? It will do you immense good if you remain silent and let others talk.

(3) What helps is not your words but your vibrations. What transforms is not your lectures but your silent prayers. So talk little to those whom you wish to help but pray for them again and again.

(4) Always keep clear of the desire of telling others of your life and achievements, inner struggles and experiences, opinions and aspirations. Live and grow in the thought that you are as a tiny particle of dust and that no one cares for what you think or say, nor misses you when you are away.

(5) Your real value lies not in your outer, empirical self but in your inner, imperishable Self. This inner Self cares not for the applause of others. It is firmly established in Itself. Cultivate friendship with this inner Self.

(6) With love in your heart, walk the way of the helpers and servers of the children of God. The poor, the weak, the sinners, the lonely and the lost, the bird and the beast, too, are His children. Do at least one good turn every day. And remember that he who turns from the road to rescue another turns towards his goal. He who lifts the burden of the weary lightens his own load! He who speaks a word of hope to those who are in sorrow, heals his own hurt!

"Practice these six things for a week and notice the change that comes over you!"

VI

Putting Others First

By Eknath Easwaran

My grandmother was a remarkable woman. We come from a tradition that has been matriarchal for centuries, and within our large extended family of over a hundred people—Granny had weighty responsibilities. She liked to get up before dawn, long before the heat of the tropical sun became oppressive, and though I don't remember her doing anything just for herself, she would work throughout the day. Self-reliant, afraid of nothing, she stood steady as a pillar when a crisis arose—a death in the family, for instance, or a failure in the crops. In worship, in work, she set an example for everyone.

But Granny knew how to play too. She could throw off her years and join the children at their games—and not just the girls either; she played hard with the boys at tag and ball, and usually got the better of us. During a particular annual festival, she liked to stand up on the bamboo and palm swing we had fashioned in the courtyard, single out one of the strongest boys, and say, "Push me as high as you can!" And up, up she would go in prodigious arcs, wood groaning from the strain, while the women gasped and we boys stared in admiration below.

Granny possessed a great secret: she knew how to put others first. If she bothered to think about her own needs, it was only after everyone else had been taken care of. I think especially of little things that mean so much to a child. On school days, she always prepared something special for my lunch—a favorite dish, a treat—and I would run all the way home to be with her. "Here comes the Malabar Express!" she would say. Then, though it wasn't her own lunch time, she would sit next to me and keep me company as I ate. One of the village priests called her "Big Mother"—I imagine because she nurtured and sustained us so well.

At one point, when I developed some illness or other, the local doctor prescribed a saltless diet for a year. Three hundred and sixty-five days without salt! I cannot convey to you what a sentence that was. In a tropical country where salt figures into almost every dish . . . . well, my school friends said, "Why don't you just throw yourself into the river?"

The day after the order had been given, I came to breakfast with a long, long face. "What's the use?" I said, staring down at my plate. Everyone gave me a look of commiseration. But what could they do? They felt helpless.

But not Granny. Serving me, she said quietly, "I am going on a saltless diet for a year too." I don't think I ever had a better breakfast.

I said Granny possessed a great secret, but that wasn't because she hid anything. The sad truth is that most people do not want this knowledge—chiefly, I think, because they fail to see the joy it brings, the sense of freedom.

One day I came home after school with something deeply disturbing on my mind: I had seen, for the first time, a child with elephantiasis. It is a terrifying disease, one that we are fortunately free of in this country. This little boy's legs had swollen badly. He walked only with great effort and, of course, he was unable to join in our games. I told my grandmother about him. "Granny, it must be awful for that boy to have elephantiasis and not be able to play."

Her face became very compassionate. She said, "Yes, everything in life will be hard for him." Then she added, "But only one in a million suffers from elephantiasis of the leg. There is a much more dreadful disease that can afflict every one of us if we don't guard ourselves against it all the time."

"What's that, Granny?"

"Elephantiasis of the ego."

The more I have pondered that remark down the years, the more perceptive it seems. Our swollen concern for ourselves, she was saying, constitutes the worst threat in life. And the teachings of every religion bear her out. Repeatedly we are told that ego or self-will, our drive to be separate from the wholeness of creation, is the source of all our suffering. It keeps us from accepting others, from sympathy and quick understanding. More than that, it alienates us from the supreme reality we call God. It alone prevents us from knowing that, as Meher Baba put it, "You and I are not 'we'; you and I are one."

Puffed up by our self-will, we look out at the world through the distorting medium of our likes and dislikes, hopes and fears, opinions and judgments. We want everyone to behave as we think they should—the right way. When, naturally enough, they not only behave their own way but expect us to do as they do, we get agitated. And what we see through this agitation makes up our everyday reality.

Abandoning Self-will

The word ego, as you may know, comes from the Latin for "I." Sanskrit too has a precise term for self-will: *ahaṁkāra* , from *ahaṁ*, "I," and *kāra*, "maker." *Ahaṁkāra* is the force that continuously creates our sense of I-ness and its close companions "me," "my," and "mine." Independent of any situation, something deep within us, as persistent as our heartbeat, constantly renews our sense of separateness. Whether we are awake or asleep, our ego goes on, though we are more conscious of it at some times than at others. Since it is always there, we think of it as our identity, and we protect it as a miser does his gold. Not only that, we expect others to treasure it, too.

Management consultants advise their executive clients to

establish priorities before they start to work. The ego creates priorities too. At the top of one of those legal-sized yellow pads it puts "To Be Taken Care Of." Below, on the first line, it writes "me." There follows a list of all its requirements, which take up most of the page. At the bottom come the needs of those around. Oh, yes, if there are time and energy and resources left over, we will give them freely to others. But by and large, we must be served first.

Ironically, this drive for self-aggrandizement has never led to happiness and never will. We cannot always have what we want; it is childish to think so. No one has the power to regulate this changing world so that he or she can continuously sing, "Everything's going my way"—if we could do so, it would only stunt our growth. I have heard that even simple organisms placed in an ideal environment—controlled temperature, plenty of food, no stress of any kind—soon perish. Luckily, no one is likely to put us in such a situation.

"For those whom ego overcomes," the Buddha says, "sufferings spread like wild grass." You must have seen crabgrass or dandelions take over a lawn. In the countryside where I live, our fields have an even fiercer threat: thistles. The first spring only a few appear. You can walk through the grass without any trouble from them, and if you don't know their ways, you may not bother to remove them. After all, the flowers are a lovely color, and who doesn't like thistle honey?

But the next year, the "stickers" have spread. Big patches stand here and there, small clusters are everywhere; you cannot cross the field without feeling their sting. And after a year or two, the whole field becomes a tangle of tall, strong thistles; it is agony to walk through.

Similarly, the Buddha tells us, self-will inevitably leads to increasing frustration and pain. What a strange situation! We desire, naturally enough, to be happy. But if we put our personal happiness at the top of the list, we only succeed in making ourselves miserable.

Spontaneity in Action

When a villager in India wants a monkey for a pet, he cuts a small hole in a fresh coconut and sets it on the ground. A monkey—usually an immature one—sees it, swings down, squeezes a paw through the tiny opening, and grabs a big fistful of the juicy kernel. Then comes a surprise: the hole is too small; both paw and food cannot come out together. But the little monkey will not let go! It simply cannot pass by a delicacy; so it hops around pitifully with a coconut dangling from its arm until the villager walks up and claims his new pet.

So it is with us. The ego lures us; its promises are so appealing that we cannot let them go. But in the end self-will entraps us, and we lose our freedom. Worse, we have found ways in the modern world to heighten our distress. Take the contemporary cult of personality. Nearly everyone wants to be visibly unique, to be charismatic, to have a dazzling personality. "Have you met Mr. Wonderful? He's witty, talented, and so good-looking!" Madison Avenue stands ready as ever to help us fulfill these aspirations with products that proclaim, "Now you can be the you you have always wanted you to be"—if, of course, you rinse your hair with Lady Nature Herbal-Protein Concentrate or splash on Le Sauvage aftershave.

"Personality" happens to be a perfect word here. It too comes from Latin: *persona*, the term for the face masks worn in ancient Greek and Roman plays. Have you seen sketches of them? How stony they look, how rigidly fixed! All the fluidity, all the spontaneity of the human countenance was missing. Whether he wore the down-turned mouth of the tragic mask or the grin of the comic, the actor was stuck with it throughout the play.

Our much-valued personalities are usually just like that—rigid and inflexible. We work up a particular concept of who we are and strive to live it whatever the circumstances. We think of ourselves as hard-boiled and commanding, and act harshly when we should be tender. Or we think of ourselves as kind-hearted and behave sentimentally when we should be firm.

Those old masks amplified the voice so it could be heard throughout a vast amphitheater. That was good; the Greek playwrights were worth listening to. Not long ago I was walking with some friends when along came a car with a public address system attached to the top. "Hello!" boomed a smug, disembodied voice. "I'll bet you're surprised to hear me talking to you!" Hundreds of watts of power and the fellow had nothing to say!

We may not actually carry around a public address system, but most of us want our personality to be widely known and admired. If people do not think of us—and think well of us—a good part of the time, something must be amiss, and we turn to a course, a book, a therapy, a health spa, or a different hairstyle.

This desire for attention not only leads us into affectations of dress, speech, and gesture; it also divides our consciousness. A small portion of our mind may be aware of the needs of others, but the larger portion is preoccupied with the effects we are creating. If the role does not fit, we will be self-conscious and ill at ease, never quite sure if we are going to be booed off the stage.

Surprisingly, when we stop trying to live up to an artificial image of ourselves, our real personality bursts forth—vivid, appealing, unique. Look at the lives of the great mystics—Francis of Assisi, Teresa of Avila, Sri Ramakrishna, Mahatma Gandhi. These are not drab figures stamped from the same mold; never has human personality been more dynamic, more spontaneous, more joyful, more strikingly individual. Saint Teresa, for example, underwent severe trials in setting up her order of Carmelites, but about her always hovered a wonderful playfulness. When the bell rang for recreation in the convent at Salamanca, the novices used to rush to block Teresa's way, gently tugging at her habit and cajoling her, "Mother?" "Dear Mother!" "Isn't Your Reverence staying with us?" She would laugh and yield, tarrying to compose some *coplas* which the whole convent sang, all clapping hands and dancing together.

Next to someone like this, for whom joy became a continuous presence, it is we whose lives must seem uniform and routine. No wonder Traherne says, "Till you can sing and rejoice and delight in God as misers do in gold and kings in scepters, you never enjoy the world!"

It is only by giving up this attempt to put ourselves first that we can find what we really want—peace of mind, lasting relationships, love. Do you remember the children's game "King of the Mountain"—scrambling up the sand pile, pulling and pushing each other to get on top? That may be all right when we are seven years old, but when we are twenty-seven, or fifty-seven? By the time we become adults, we should begin to think of leaving these scrambling games behind.

Eradicating self-will is the means by which we realize the supreme goal of the spiritual life. This is what all the great mystics have done, and done completely, through years of strenuous effort. True, if we set out to do it, we are going to find it difficult and uncomfortable for a long while. But what freedom we experience when that monstrous impediment we call the ego is finally removed! Says Saint Bernard of Clairvaux:

> Just as air flooded with the light of the sun is transformed into the same splendor of light, so that it appears not so much lighted up as to be light itself; so it will inevitably happen that every human affection will then, in some ineffable manner, melt away from self and be entirely transfused . . . . The substance indeed will remain, but in another form, another glory, and another power . . . .

In this self-naughting lies the power of life itself, and through it we are born anew. This is what Jesus meant when he said, "If you want to find your life, you have to lose it." It is what Gandhi meant when he said, in response to the suggestion that he was without ambition: "Oh, no, I have the greatest ambition imaginable. I want to make myself zero."

What concrete steps can we take to bring this about? What

can we do day by day?

When my grandmother told me about elephantiasis of the ego, I remember I asked her whether there was any cure for this malady. "Oh, yes," she said. "Love of God."

Love of God? Some may say it was natural that Granny would use those words, with her devotional Hindu background. You might even hear them among a few pious people in the West. But what can they possibly mean to us? If the materialistic bent of our culture has not banished such devotion, our intellectual training has. How can we conceivably have a fervent love of God in our times? It is a good question, and I think there is a practical answer to it.

First, we need to ask what we mean by "love." The term that has been used so shamelessly in connection with all kinds of things—soft drinks, paper towels, garage door openers. And love between a man and a woman, we are told, means a muscular, tanned fellow running hand in hand through the surf with a stunning, billowy-haired girl, or couples sitting across glasses of wine at a little hideaway restaurant. From such imagery we draw our romantic notions of love.

But listen to Saint Paul, in his First Letter to the Corinthians:

> Love is patient; love is kind and envies no one. Love is never boastful, nor conceited, nor rude; never selfish, not quick to take offense. Love keeps no score of wrongs; does not gloat over others' sins, but delights in the truth. There is nothing love cannot face; there is no limit to its faith, its hope, and its endurance. Love will never come to an end.

That is a love worthy of us. That is a love powerful enough to dissolve our self-will. When Jesus urged us to love God, he added also: "Thou shalt love thy neighbor as thyself." The two interconnect. The Lord is present in every one of us, and when we love those around us, we are loving Him. The Hindu scriptures put it memorably:

> When a man loves his wife more than himself, he is loving the Lord in her. When a woman loves her husband more than

herself, she is loving the Lord in him. When parents love their children more than themselves, they are loving the Lord in them.

Everyone Can Learn to Love

I once spoke to a group of high school girls at a luncheon in Minneapolis. After my talk I answered questions, and the girl who presided asked, "You've used the word love many times. What does love mean to you?" I gave her the same answer: "When your boyfriend's welfare means more to you than your own, you are in love." This girl turned to the rest of the gathering and said candidly, "Well, I guess none of us has ever been in love."

I think that can be said for most people. But we can learn to be in love. The spiritual life is marvelously fair: it is open to everybody. No favoritism, no hereditary class. No matter where you start, you can learn everything you need to learn, provided you are prepared to work at it. So too of love. Any one of us may be very self-willed now, but why should we be depressed about it? We can begin the work of eradicating our self-will, and the easiest and most natural way is by putting the welfare of those around us first.

In a sense, it comes down to attention. When we are preoccupied with ourselves—our thoughts, our desires, our preferences—we cannot help becoming insensitive to others' needs. We can pay attention only to so much, and all our attention rests on ourselves. When we turn away from ourselves, even if only a little, we begin to see what is really best for those we love.

Hugh, for instance, really looks forward to watching "The Wide World of Sports" every weekend. He has done it for years. "I've had a hard week," he says, puts up his stockinged feet on the ottoman, and leans back.

But what about his wife, Elaine? Was her week so easy? He might ask her what she would like to do. Go to the beach? Shop?

Get the garden started? It might be painful to pry himself away, but if he loves her and if he wants to grow—he will choose to read the scores in Monday's paper.

For Hugh it may be "The Wide World of Sports" that has to be forgone; for another it may be a shopping trip, a nap, a chance to make some extra money, a hobby, an unfinished painting. Whatever it is, giving it up, even temporarily, may hurt. Our preferences are sticky, like the adhesive on a bandage; there may be a wince when we tear them away. But it has to be done if we want to relate easily and lovingly with those around.

Any time we refrain from self-centered ways of acting, speaking and even thinking, we are putting others first. Anger, for example, is often nothing more than violated self-will. Hugh expected a bonus and didn't get it, so he sulks. Elaine wants their son Jack to stop tinkering with his car and spend more time on his schoolwork, but Jack has other ideas; both get resentful and quarrel. To be blunt, when we are crossed like this by people or events, we do our human equivalent of roaring, baring our fangs, and lashing out with claw, horn, tail, or hoof. The household can become quite a menagerie.

But anger is power, and Hugh, Elaine, and all the rest of us can learn to harness this power by putting each other first. Whatever the flavor of our anger—irritability, rage, stubbornness, belligerence, or sullen silence—it can all be transformed into compassion and understanding. Those we live with will certainly benefit from that, and so will we.

This does not mean that if someone we love tries to do something foolish or injurious, we should ignore it or connive at it by saying, "Whatever you want, dear." Putting others first does not at all entail making ourselves into a doormat. In fact, if we really love someone, we will find it necessary to speak out for that person's real and long-term interest—even to the point of loving, tender, but firm opposition.

Often the way we do this makes all the difference. If we are accusing or resentful we will seem entangled, judgmental, just the opposite of loving. Our words, our facial expressions, may betray a lack of respect: "I knew you couldn't stay on that diet, Hugh!" Even with the best of conscious intentions, we may provoke a nasty clash. But if we can support the other person and express our disapproval tenderly, with respect, it will help him or her to see more clearly. When we have such a helpmate, my grandmother used to say, we do not need a mirror.

Lately I have run across bestselling books encouraging people to compete with each other, even with one's own husband or wife. Many couples, I hear, have taken this advice. Who brings home the most income? Who has the most promising career? I have even seen couples compete over their friends— or, tragically, for the love of their own children. But a man and woman brought into union are not adversaries. They are meant to complete each other, not to compete. Their union should dissolve separate boundaries—what is bad for one can never be good for the other.

Patience

In my experience, love can be fairly well summed up in a single word: patience. Oh, I know it isn't thought to be a glamorous quality. I don't remember anyone writing a song about it. We can turn on the radio and hear songs about coral lips and pearly teeth, about candlelight and moonlight, about Paris and Rio . . . nothing about patience. But you can have very ordinary lips and uneven teeth, live in Hoboken and never travel, and still have the most ardent love affair with your husband or wife, boyfriend or girlfriend, if you both have patience.

Just try flying off to Acapulco with the current sex symbol and see how well you get on if you are both impatient! For a few dazzling hours you may be able to conceal from one another the self-will lurking within. Even after the puzzled glances, the astonished stares, the little disagreements begin, you can still ignore them by searching out a new wine to savor, a new sight to see. But soon the truth becomes painfully clear to all parties, and before long you are on the phone: "Flight to the States, please—any flight! For one, one way."

When you are patient, on the other hand, an unkind word or thoughtless act will not agitate you. You will not want to run away or retaliate. Your support will hold steady, based as it is on deep respect and the knowledge that the Lord lives in the other person. Pride will not keep you from making the first—and, if need be, the second or third—overture towards reconciliation.

The scriptures of all religions contrast spiritual union with the relationship based solely on physical attraction. The first shows itself in patience and forgiveness; each person wants what is best for the other. The second cannot help being evanescent, marked by manipulation, self-assertion, and pride, because each person wants what is pleasurable for himself or herself.

We need not talk about right and wrong here at all. I am saying, simply and practically, that while sex has a beautiful place where loyalty exists, we cannot build a lasting relationship on it. The very nature of the physical bond is to exhaust itself quickly. One day we think Cecily or Dexter the most flawless, the most alluring creature on earth; we cannot live another moment apart from such embodied charm. This is the stuff of great literature—all those stories and poems which depict the suffering lover. But some months later, isn't most or all of that gone? Strange, but when we look closely, Cecily has some not so endearing quirks of personality that we never noticed before; Dexter's physical imperfections have begun to grate on our nerves. And there we are: alone again, lonely, perhaps moving on to Angelique or Zachary . . . who (and this time we couldn't be wrong) is the most flawless and alluring creature on earth.

I am not denying the temporary satisfaction in a relationship centered only on sex. That is what pulls us into it. But if we follow that pull, we are heading for disruption, and for all the heartbreak and turmoil that follow. If we want relationships that deepen with the passage of time, relationships that help us grow, we have to remain loyal through the bad times as well as the good, to accept the differences as well as the congruencies. This is what we learn to do when we try patiently to put the other person first.

VII

The Relinquishments

By Peace Pilgrim

[*The following excerpt is taken from the book* Peace Pilgrim. *In Chapter II, Peace Pilgrim outlines her spiritual practices such as Preparations, Purifications, and Relinquishments which helped her leave the self-centered life.*]

Once you've made the first relinquishment you have found inner peace, because it's *the relinquishment of self-will.*

You can work on subordinating the lower self by refraining from doing the not-good things you may be motivated toward—not suppressing them—but transforming them so that the higher Self can take over your life. If you are motivated to do or say a mean thing, you can always think of a good thing. You deliberately turn around and use that *same energy* to do or say a good thing instead. It works!

The second relinquishment is *the relinquishment of the feeling of separateness.* We begin feeling very separate and judging everything as it relates to us, as though we were the center of the universe. Even after we know better intellectually, we still judge things that way. In reality, of course, we are all cells in the body of humanity. We are not separate from our fellow humans. The whole thing is a totality. It's only from that higher viewpoint that you can know what it is to love your neighbor as yourself. From that higher viewpoint there becomes just one realistic way to work, and that is for the good of the whole. As long as you work for your selfish little self, you're just one cell against all those other cells, and you're way out of harmony. But as soon as you begin working for the good of the whole, you find yourself in harmony with all of your fellow human beings. You see, it's the easy, harmonious way to live.

Then there is the third relinquishment, and that is *the relinquishment of all attachments.* No one is truly free who is still attached to material things, or to places, or to people. Material things must be put into their proper place. They are there for use. It's all right to use them, that's what they're there for. But when they've outlived their usefulness, be ready to relinquish them and perhaps pass them on to someone who does need them. Anything that you cannot relinquish when it has outlived its usefulness possesses you, and in this materialistic age a great many of us are possessed by our possessions. We are not free.

I considered myself liberated long before it became the fashion. First I liberated myself from debilitating habits, and went on to free myself of combative, aggressive thoughts. I have also cast aside any unnecessary possessions. This, I feel, is true liberation.

There is another kind of possessiveness. You do not possess any other human being, no matter how closely related that other may be. No husband owns his wife; no wife owns her husband; no parents own their children. When we think we possess people there is a tendency to run their lives for them, and out of this develop extremely inharmonious situations. Only when we realize that we do not possess them, that they must live in accordance with their own inner motivations, do we stop trying to run their lives for them, and then we discover that we are able to live in harmony with them. Anything that you strive to hold captive will hold you captive—and if you desire freedom you must give freedom.

Associations formed in this earth life are not necessarily for the duration of the life span. Separation takes place constantly, and as long as it takes place *lovingly,* not only is there no spiritual injury, but spiritual progress may actually be helped.

We must be able to appreciate and enjoy the places where we tarry and yet pass on without anguish when we are called elsewhere. In our spiritual development, we are often required to pull up roots many times, and to close many chapters in our lives until we are no longer attached to any material thing and can love all people without any attachment to them.

Now the last relinquishment: *the relinquishment of all negative feelings*. I want to mention just one negative feeling which the nicest people still experience, and that negative feeling is *worry*. Worry is not *concern,* which would motivate you to do everything possible in a situation. Worry is a useless mulling over of things we cannot change.

One final comment about negative feelings, which helped me very much at one time and has helped others. No outward thing—nothing, nobody from without—can hurt me inside, psychologically. I recognized that I could only be hurt psychologically by my own wrong actions, which I have control over; by my own wrong *reactions* (they are tricky, but I have control over them too); or by my own *inaction* in some situations, like the present world situation, that needs action from me. When I recognized all this how free I felt! And I just stopped hurting myself. Now someone could do the meanest thing to me and I would feel deep compassion for this out-of-harmony person, this sick person, who is capable of doing mean things. I certainly would not hurt myself by a wrong reaction of bitterness or anger. You have complete control over whether you will be psychologically hurt or not, and anytime you want to, you can stop hurting yourself.

Finding Harmony Within

These are my steps toward inner peace that I wanted to share with you. There is nothing new about this. This is universal truth. I merely talked about these things in everyday words in terms of my own personal experience with them. The laws which govern this universe work for good as soon as we obey them, and anything contrary to these laws does not last long. It contains within itself the seeds of its own destruction. The good in every human life always makes it possible for us to obey these laws. We do have free will about all this, and therefore how soon we obey and thereby find harmony, both within ourselves and within our world, is up to us.

During this spiritual growing up period I desired to know and do God's will for me. Spiritual growth is not easily attained, but it is well worth the effort. It takes time, just as any growth takes time. One should rejoice at small gains and not be impatient, as impatience hampers growth.

The path of gradual relinquishment of things hindering spiritual progress is a difficult path, for only when relinquishment is complete do the rewards really come. The path of quick relinquishment is an easy path, for it brings immediate blessings. And when God fills your life, God's gifts overflow to bless all you touch.

To me, it was an escape from the artificiality of illusion into the richness of reality. To the world it may seem that I had given up much. I had given up burdensome possessions, spending time meaninglessly, doing things I knew I should not do, and not doing things I knew I should do. But to me it seemed that I had gained much—even the priceless treasures of health and happiness.

VIII

Letters to Devotees

by Swami Turiyananda

[The following article was taken from Spiritual Treasures, *which contain letters by Swami Turiyananda, a disciple of Sri Ramakrishna. The letters were translated and edited by Swami Chetanananda.]*

Kankhal
27 September 1913
Dear X,

I have received your letter of 4 Aswin [September 1913]. . . .

I am glad to hear that you have enjoyed my comments on the *Bhagavad Gītā.* The import of verse 27, Chapter 9, "Whatever you do or eat, and so on," which you have written, is correct. The idea is to think of oneself as an instrument and God as the doer. There is another idea: He has become everything, and He plays all these games while residing in every being. Like this, there can be so many interpretations. All of these attitudes demand the cessation of this puny "I." Know for certain that this petty ego is the root of all troubles and ignorance.

Self-surrender means: To practice contentment by thinking that wherever the Lord keeps me is for my good; to unify one's will with the will of God; and to practice even-mindedness in happiness and misery, gain and loss, and so on. In other words, one can surrender oneself completely only after liberation. Before that one will have to practice yoga repeatedly. Real resignation to God is liberation. If a person practices this attitude of resignation sincerely and wholeheartedly, he attains liberation by God's grace.

You have mentioned renunciation. In this context, the Master used to say: "A housewife at first does all sorts of toilsome work; but when she becomes pregnant, her mother-in-law gradually curtails her work and does not allow her to do very much. At last when she brings forth a baby, she is released from all work. Her only work then is to stay with the baby and nurse him; and the happiness of the baby becomes her happiness." Now pregnancy means to install God in one's heart, and giving birth to a child means God-realization.

There is another attitude: Stay at the door of the Lord and wait for His grace. If you are sincere, divine grace will be bestowed on you. The Master explained it through the parable of the kitten. It neither desires something different nor attempts to do anything on its own; wherever its mother keeps it, it remains there. To have perfection in any one of these *sādhanā-s*—that is the only thing needed. The Lord is omniscient. He knows each and all. "As your faith, so is your attainment.". . .

With love,

Turiyananda

* * *

Kankhal

10 September 1914

Dear X,

. . . Hold this idea constantly in your mind: "Within me art Thou; outside me art Thou. I am the machine; Thou art the operator. I act according to Thy bidding." What more is needed? Can it be achieved by one stroke? Practice is necessary and through repeated practice comes success. God will then truly be the operator of the body. This is a fact: "By some artifice the Divine Mother remains bound by the cord of devotion." She is doing everything. Incapable of understanding this, we think we are the doers and thus get bound by action. Suppose a person is cooking rice in a pot with potatoes and other vegetables. After a while, when the vegetables begin to toss to and fro, children think that the vegetables are jumping. But those who understand say that it appears that way because of the fire below the pot. Take the fire away and everything will be quiet. Likewise, God is doing everything, residing within us as the power of consciousness and the power of action. Unable to understand this, we say we are the doers.

Is there anyone but the Lord in this universe? It is He alone who is manifested in different forms. Because of our ignorance we see many things in place of Him. If one can perceive Him, one will not see diversity anymore and will not suffer. He is within everyone. He is everything. When one is established in this knowledge, one becomes free.

In the *Vyādha-Gītā* of the *Mahābhārata*, the hunter had attained knowledge in his previous birth, but due to *prārabdha karma* [the results of past action] he was born as a hunter. He followed his duty according to his caste, but he himself would not kill any animals. He used to buy meat from others and sell it in the market. This is what we find in the *Mahābhārata*.

You have quoted from the *Gītā*: "He who is free from the feeling of I-consciousness and whose understanding is undefiled—though he slays these men, he slays not nor is he bound."[1] If you reflect a little you will understand: when a person does not have any ego-sense or think "I am the doer," there cannot be any bondage. It is the sense of "I" that binds. "When shall I be free? When I will cease to be." If there is no "I," where is the bondage? "Not I, not I, but Thou, Thou." He who has no ego-sense sees God only. So he is not bound. . . .

Yours,

Turiyananda

* * *

Lord's Grace!

Almora
10 December 1915
Dear L,

I was glad to receive your letter of December 3 . . . .

It is very difficult all at once to feel the presence of God in every being; it is not entirely possible unless one attains illumination. But God is all-pervading, and dwells in all beings—knowing this, if a person serves human beings, he is serving God also. If one can serve in this spirit wholeheartedly and without desiring the fruits of one's action, through the grace of the Lord one will realize in time that service to man is worship of God. For the Lord is present in every being: truly, He alone exists.

Purity and impurity are nothing but differences in one's attitude. Attachment to sense objects is impurity, and attachment to God is purity. That which is real in human beings is God. Without God, man is nothing but a cage of flesh and bones. The consciousness in man is a part of God, and that is pure: everything else is impure. The good tendencies in man lead him towards God, and the bad tendencies keep him away from God. One can understand this gradually, but in the beginning of *sādhanā* one should hear about it.

It is only through the grace of God that one is drawn to having a good character. God is the source of all goodness. Therefore, realizing God, one gets rid of restlessness and becomes blessed by attaining supreme peace. What is needed is that you steadfastly keep waiting at His door, and the Lord will reveal everything to you. Always maintain good tendencies in your heart. God is goodness itself. If you can keep Him in your heart, you will lack nothing whatsoever. God is our mother and father, friend and companion, wealth and wisdom—He is our all in all. Thus if you can make Him your own, your life will be blissful.

You have asked too many questions; it is not possible to

answer all of them. And even if I did answer them, I don't think you would be able to understand. But this is certain: The more you move towards Him, the more your understanding will be clarified, and thus all of your problems will be solved. Without having a spiritual mood within, one cannot understand spiritual ideas.

Always try to see the Lord within your heart. When you need to know anything, ask Him with utmost sincerity. From within, He will make you know everything; He always does that for everybody. If God does not reveal himself, with all one's efforts, one can neither understand nor help another to understand. What seems to you now a great mystery will become clear very easily through His grace, and you will see the truth. It takes time; don't be impatient. Call on God with all your heart and soul, and try to make Him your own. Pray to the Lord from the depth of your being. He is omniscient. Knowing our intentions, He arranges everything accordingly. There is no doubt about it. With love and best wishes,
Turiyananda

* * *

12 December 1915
Dear Baburam Maharaj [Swami Premananda],

I was extremely delighted to receive your letter of December 1, 1915. . . .

Love is a great power—there is no doubt about it. To pray for the welfare of others, to wish that they may have peace, that they may reach the source of joy—if these desires are a cause of bondage then that bondage is of divine love. It will break the bondage of the world, lead one to immortality and make one blessed. Please bless us that we may have the privilege of getting even a particle of that love. . . .
With love and salutations,
Turiyananda

* * *

Almora
1 June 1916
Dear Prajnananda,

Now the question of spiritual practice—meditation and concentration, *japaṁ* (repetition of the Lord's name) and austerity, worship and study of the scriptures, yoga and Vedic ritual—all these actions or *sādhanā-s* are only meant for purification of the mind. And the purpose of purifying the mind is Self-realization or Self-knowledge. The mind becomes impure when it is swarming with desires and becomes pure when it is free from desires. Now the main task is to make the mind unselfish by any means—whether it is through meditation, service, discrimination, or devotion. Everyone has his own choice. But everybody will have to destroy the ego. And when this "little ego" dissolves, one experiences the manifestation of the "Cosmic Ego," or *Brahman*. This is called *jīvanmukti*, or freedom while living in the body.

The grace of the Lord is always there; it is never absent. When the mind is purified, one experiences and tastes fully that divine grace. Self-knowledge is ever-existent; it has no past or future. The sun appears when the cloud is blown away. Similarly, when ignorance is removed, the self-luminous, ever-present Self manifests. People do so many things to attain this Self-knowledge, but *śraddhā* or unswerving faith, is the most important prerequisite. The *Gītā* says, "He who is full of faith and zeal and has subdued his senses obtains knowledge."[2] . . .
Your well-wisher,
Turiyananda

* * *

True Renunciation

Sashi Niketan
Puri
21 July 1917
Dear D,

I am pleased to receive your letter of Shravan 1 [July 1917]. I was extremely delighted to learn from your letter that the Lord is inspiring you with good thoughts, and that your mind is becoming purer and purer. May He bless you more, that is my sincere prayer to Him.

Truly, it is not easy to get rid of all desires, but if the mind is endowed with discrimination, then desires cannot overpower it. The sage Vashishtha told Ramachandra, "If one has discrimination, then even in a great crisis one is unperturbed." Indeed the power of delusion cannot overwhelm if one can keep the discriminative faculty ever steady. What harm can desire do to that person who always thinks that everything is transitory? There is nothing to fear from trifling desires. That desire is really harmful which takes the mind away from God. If the mind is fixed on God, cravings cannot mislead a person even if he is in family life. Pray to God and open your heart to Him; He will set everything right.

There is a beautiful story in the *Yoga Vaśiṣṭha Rāmāyaṇa* about renunciation. A *brahmacārī* [young monk], considering himself a man of renunciation, gave up everything except a piece of loincloth, an *āsana* [carpet for meditation], and a water pot. In order to give him right understanding, his guru said to him: "What have you renounced? I see that you have renounced nothing." The *brahmacārī* thought: "I have nothing except this loincloth, *āsana*, and water pot. Does my guru want me to give up these things?" Deliberating thus, he kindled a fire and one by one threw those possessions into it. He then felt that he had achieved true renunciation. The guru said: "What have you renounced? A piece of cloth? It is made of cotton. Your *āsana* and water pot are also made with different materials. All of these materials belong to nature. What have you renounced of your own?" Then the *brahmacārī* pondered: "What else do I have? Of course, I have my own body. Well, I shall sacrifice this body into the fire." When the *brahmacārī* was about to throw himself into the flames, the guru said: "Wait a minute. What are you doing? Just reason it out: Does this body belong to you? This body was made by your parents with their semen and blood, and later it grew from the nourishment of food. What has it got to do with you?" Then the *brahmacārī* finally came to his senses. Through the grace of the guru he realized that his ego was the root of all evil. Real renunciation is the renunciation of ego; otherwise, renunciation of external things, even one's own body, is not considered to be renunciation.

Therefore, taking or giving up—these pairs of opposites are futile because they are in the domain of *māyā*. The essential thing in life is to take refuge in God. One should pray for one-pointed devotion, love of His devotees, and a taste for His name. . . .

Your well-wisher,
Turiyananda

* * *

Shashi Niketan
Puri
7 September 1917
Dear Nirmal [Swami Madhavananda],

I have received your letter of August 28 . . . .

In the beginning one has to understand the Truth through discrimination. Afterwards, when that discrimination becomes firm and free from doubt, realization takes place immediately. Whenever there is a cessation of doubt, misgiving, and contrary notions with regard to Truth, the mind becomes firmly settled on the Self. This is called the realization of Truth. Through the grace of the Lord "one attains It within himself in due course."

Today I have received a postcard from M. Tell him that one

cannot get rid of egoism simply by not doing anything. The way to do this lies through work. If you want to fry something, you must use fire to heat the oil. To refine sugar you have to remove a lot of scum by boiling it. Likewise, if you want to purify your mind, you will have to perform action without seeking its results. It [purification] cannot be achieved by withdrawing one's hands and feet like a tortoise. "I won't work because it may cause pride" this attitude springs from sheer selfishness. It is a sign of a dreadful *tāmasika* (sluggish) nature. One must convert *tamas* into *rajas* (activity) through work, and then gradually it will be transformed into *sattva* (calm) through spiritual disciplines, thus will the ego be driven out.

One who has no sense of ego is not the doer, although he may be engaged in work. One who harbors a feeling of pride will be proud even when he is idle. And one who is humble and calm does not feel that he is doing anything, although he does many things. . . .

With love and best wishes,
Turiyananda

* * *

Varanasi
31 May 1920
Dear Gurudas [Gupta],

I was pleased to receive your letter of May 28. It is not a small thing that gradually you are becoming more aware of yourself. Thus you continue your journey from outside to inside and gradually reach the inmost Self. If you can experience your true nature, then the purpose of your life will be over. Your life will be blessed attaining that state: "It is the Ear of the ear, the Mind of the mind, the Speech of speech, the Life of life, and the Eye of the eye. Having detached the Self [from the sense organs] and renounced the world, the wise attain Immortality."[3] Experiencing the Self in all, "he cannot hate anyone."[4]

As long as one has a connection with the body, senses, and mind one has knowledge of good and bad. When one is strongly connected with the Supreme Self, the pairs of opposites do not exist. In other words, good and bad cannot perturb one anymore. "If a person knows the Self as *I am this,* then desiring what and for whose sake will he suffer in the wake of the body?"[5] If a person has the knowledge "I am the *Ātman,*" then in spite of physical and mental afflictions he can remain in bliss experiencing his true nature. As he has separated himself from his body and mind, their afflictions do not affect him.

Thinking "I am the body, I am the body," I become identified with the body. Then why should I not be identified with the *Ātman* if I think "I am the *Ātman,* I am the *Ātman?*" The cause of our suffering is the acceptance of untruth as truth. If we could know the truth as truth, then all of our misery would go away and happiness would come to us. To experience the Truth, one needs long practice with infinite patience. Practice and renunciation are the main supports. If one has steadfast devotion, everything becomes easy by God's grace.

The study of the *Gītā* will help you to understand the Truth easily. "O *Bhagavad Gītā,* you destroy man's rebirth in this mortal world. O Mother, I meditate on you." [Meditation of the *Gītā,* verse 1] What more is there to say? This is the goal in life as well as in death.

Never forget these sayings of the Master: "One matchstick can destroy one hundred years' darkness in a moment. One drop of God's grace removes all ignorance which accumulated through birth after birth." Longing is essential because it quickly leads to perfection. In fact, I am really happy, knowing you are making good progress.

FOOTNOTES:

[1.] *Bhagavad Gītā,* XVIII:17.
[2.] *Ibid.,* IV:39.
[3.] *Kena Upaniṣad,* 1.2.
[4.] *Īśā Upaniṣad,* 81.
[5.] *Bṛhadāraṇyaka Upaniṣad,* IV.4.121.

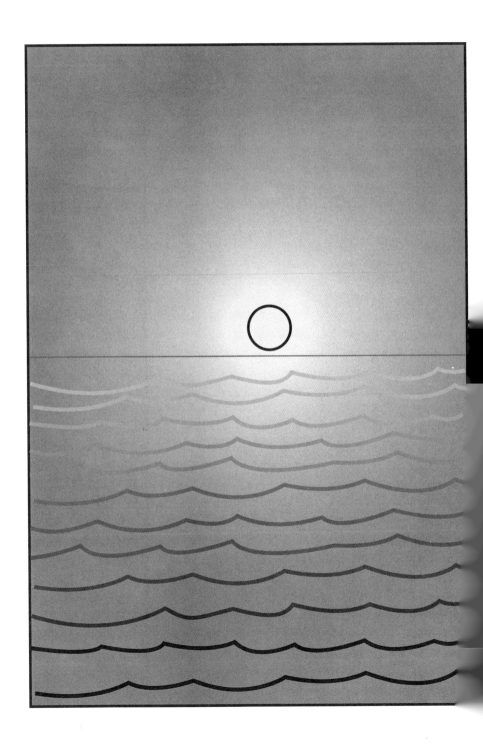

PART THREE

Going Beyond

*Change thy thought from the world
and cast it wholly on Him
and He shall nourish thee.*

Richard Rolle

Those who have overcome self-will and become instruments to do God's work can accomplish tasks which are seemingly impossible, but they experience no feeling of self-achievement. I now know myself to be a part of the infinite cosmos, not separate from other souls or God. My illusory self is dead; the real Self controls the garment of clay and uses it for God's work. . . .

Any praise I receive does not change me, for I pass it right along to God. I walk, because God gives me the strength to walk, I live because God gives me the supply to live, I speak because God gives me the words to speak. All I did was to surrender my will to God's will. . . . I do my work easily and joyously. I feel beauty all around me and I see beauty in everyone I meet, for I see God in everything.

Peace Pilgrim

IX

Overcoming the Ego

by Swami Ramdas

Q: Does the spiritual quest occasionally reinforce the sense of ego?

A: Yes, if you think highly of yourself after making a little progress on the spiritual path. That is the main pitfall on the path of spirituality. Those who have advanced a bit think that they have advanced a lot. Spiritual progress must gradually eliminate the ego-sense and make the aspirant more and more humble. Instead of that, after some practice, some people think that they are big and superior to others. This is the danger. They must become humble and see defects in others less and less until they have that equal vision in which they see only God everywhere. In that vision there is no sense of superiority or inferiority. It is so pure and glorious. That is the state in which you transcend good and evil, likes and dislikes. This is called *samatā*. There are no waves rising and falling in the mind. It is completely at a standstill, through which divine power and joy reveal themselves.

Q: In our desire for peace, is there not a subtle danger of the same kind, a desire for self-seeking?

A: You know that to desire for things of the world is like adding fuel to the fire. And yet, you go on increasing your longing for the things of the world. But when the desire for God gets a strong hold on you, and you earnestly seek Him, your desires for worldly enjoyments gradually diminish and you become desireless. The desire to realize God is to become desireless. When you become desireless, you are really free. A person who is bound by many desires is in a state of terrible bondage, and that is the cause of his living under limitations and getting his individuality strengthened, with the result that he feels he is separate from the rest of existence. Thereby he is subject to likes and dislikes, good and evil, sin and virtue, and many other pairs of opposites which keep him always in a state of turmoil, unrest, and discontentment. If you want to free yourself from these opposites, it is necessary that the ego-sense disappears. So, aspiration for God should make you free from all desires.

Repetition of the Name

Q: Is the desire to become desireless not a subtle form of the ego-sense?

A: The ego does not die in the very beginning, you have to overcome it. This means the ego must be made to desire to be desireless. Give it the name of God to repeat, and the ego will gradually grow thin and finally disappear.

Q: Is there no chance of the ego keeping something for itself?

A: Ramdas will tell you a story. A man wanted to propitiate a devil in order to make it do whatever he wanted. Therefore he did the necessary practice toward that end, and by the power of some mantra and other disciplines, he was able to summon the devil before him. The devil said that it would obey his commands, but on one condition: "If at any time you do not give me work, I will devour you. You must keep me engaged all the twenty-four hours." The man agreed. He immediately gave an order for a palace to be built. To his great wonder, the palace was built in no time. Then he gave an order to make a long road. That work was also executed very quickly. The next minute the devil was standing before him, asking for more work. He had no time to think. He gave an order to build a big town. It was ready in ten minutes. He gave another order for a still bigger town. That was built in twenty minutes. Now the man was perplexed and afraid. He did not know what order to give next. If he did not give any work, he would be swallowed by the devil. He hastened to a holy man and asked for advice and the holy man suggested that he should get a bamboo pole, plant it in the ground and ask the devil to climb up and down it until further orders. He did so and as the devil was bound to carry out the order, it meant no rest whatever for the devil. The devil got disgusted and ran away.

Now, in your case, *Ram mantra* (repetition of the Lord's name) is the pole, and the ego is the devil that teases you. Ask him to go up and down the pole repeatedly and he will soon get disgusted and run away. The name of *Ram* is given to you in order to make the ego disappear. He must be made to disappear by his own effort. The principle of repeating the Name lies in this. As you continue repeating the Name, your ego-sense becomes thinner and thinner and ultimately disappears. Then you realize that you are the all-pervading Spirit. If you try to bring out by the power of the Name the source of sweetness and joy hidden within you, then, naturally, all that is not divine in you will disappear and all that is divine in you will manifest itself as love, joy, and power.

The Indian sages say that the ego does not exist at all. According to their experience, God alone exists. The sense of ego or ego-consciousness—not ego as such—is responsible for feeling that we are separate from God, though we really are not. Sheer ignorance has captured us, and when this ignorance goes, we shall know what we are in reality. This is not a new attainment. It is only the regaining of the knowledge of what we are. Something is in us which we have forgotten, but once we remember it and discover it, we know it was with us even before. So our union and oneness with God is eternally there. According to Hindu teachings, ignorance is the cause of our bondage. Ignorance consists in not knowing what we are.

An example is often given of what happens in the ordinary course of our lives. A normally happy person suddenly feels unhappy when a particle of dust falls into his eyes. He has irritation and pain and therefore feels very uncomfortable. He goes to the doctor and gets the particle of dust removed. Now he says he is happy. Is it a new happiness that he gets? No, he regains only that which he had lost. Before the dust fell into his eyes he was happy, the dust caused temporary unhappiness and when it was removed he regained that happiness. This is how the saints of India teach. It is not that you attain anything new when you realize God. You have been God, you are God, and you will be God.

Beyond the Mind

Q: When our mind has been destroyed, how can we go on acting in the world, doing good deeds and so on?

A: It is true that when the mind is destroyed, we are then imbued with the power of God. Activity will go on with the power of God. We know now it is He who makes us do everything. When we are ignorant, we think we are doing everything, and that is the reason why we act wrongly. Just as canal water which flows without any muddy obstruction will be clear as crystal, and will become dirty when the obstruction is there. In the same way, when we allow a free flow of the divine power through us without the obstruction of the ego, things will go well, but when the ego-sense is present, we do evil things. When the ego-sense is gone, we realize that it is God's power alone that does everything. The whole universe, with all its beings and creatures, is moved by His power and will alone. When we know this, our ego-sense disappears. It is a mistake to think that our actions will cease when we realize God. There are great yogis whose egos have completely disappeared and who are working for the good of the world. They work for the fulfillment of the divine purpose, which is to bring harmony and peace in the world.

Q: Does that mean we will have mastered our thoughts?

A: No. We have handed ourselves over to God completely so that He may use us as He likes.

Q: Then in that case our thoughts are also divine, are they?

A: There are no thoughts there. God thinks for us. God does everything for us.

Q: Is that intuition?

A: Yes. Intuition means the prompting of God. Our thinking machinery is not at work then. As long as we still have that machinery and use it, we will always blunder.

Q: But do we still feel the duality between God and us?

A: There is duality and there is non-duality also. We can take ourselves as instruments of God. Sometimes we feel the instrument is also He. So there is duality in non-duality, and non-duality in duality. As God is everything, He must be dual as well as nondual.

Q: Can we feel that God is doing everything even if we do not act morally.

A: We cannot act immorally if we know God is making us do everything. Some people think that God is working through them, when the ego is making them do things. Actually it must become an experience with you that God works through you. Then you will never do anything wrong.

What is wrong and what is right? To do things knowing that you are one with others is right. When you feel you and others are different and do things, then it is wrong. All the wrong things are done because we think ourselves as separate from our fellow-beings. When we feel one with them we will never do wrong.

Q: What is the importance of self-surrender on the spiritual path?

A: Self-surrender means giving up of the sense of ego. We cannot realize God until the sense of ego is completely eliminated. It acts as a screen between God and us. If we remove the screen, we know that we are He.

X

Supreme Humility

Swami Jyotirmayananda

When the mind is highly fulfilled, without the pressure of the unconscious *vāsanā-s* (subtle desires), ego is transcended and one begins to experience one's unity with the Divine Self. In that state of perfection, there is an utter absence of ego, a spontaneous blossoming of supreme humility. . . .

Blessed Are the Meek

"Blessed are the meek for they shall inherit the earth." This third beatitude from Lord Jesus's *Sermon on the Mount* extols the great virtue of humility and points to its majestic power. The "meekness" referred to here is profoundly different from the "meekness" of common parlance. It is not to be confused with the dullness of mind that leads a person to simply accept without questioning whatever the world presents before him. Nor is it at all like the degrading timidity that leaves many people feeling humiliated again and again in life. Certainly it is not the feigned humility that a crafty person adopts to help him get what he wants out of a situation. Such a person may act like a sheep, but he may well be a wolf in sheep's clothing!

The blessed meekness praised by Lord Jesus is that yogic state of advanced personality integration in which one is so profoundly in tune with Cosmic Will that he has no need to assert his ego. Ever guided by the Divine hand, he carries out the will of God with total surrender, with the innocent meekness of a sheep driven by the Great Shepherd—God, the Divine Self.

The highest state of "meekness" is reached when a devotee is able to totally cast his ego-center into the ocean of the Divine Self through the intuitive realization of God. This is achieved through a mind which sees the very ego-center as merely a reflection of that Self, and not the absolute reality within.

In the lesser stages of spiritual development, the ego-center seems to be all that we have, and we are constantly trying to assert the ego. However, as we reflect deeply and inquire into "Who am I?" we gradually realize the illusoriness of the perception of ego, and the vanity involved in being a slave to egoistic consciousness. We eventually understand that the ego is not the all-important factor that it appeared to be, and the tension due to egoistic illusions gradually begins to subside.

One who has developed such meekness of spirit enjoys a unique type of relaxation, and experiences a joy that so far excels ordinary happiness that it is termed as Bliss. One's mind is no longer under the grip of selfishness, no longer tarnished by the impressions of frustrations and sorrow that accompany egoistic consciousness. The radiantly healthy mind of such a person becomes a basis for intense creative activity that can do immeasurable good for many, many people.

Mind is a form of divine energy and it is necessary that an aspirant use that energy with respect. If we use our mental energy properly and see that our mind is kept relaxed and cheerful day by day, then Nature flows through that mind creating wonders. We begin to think powerful thoughts that we would never have imagined possible. We begin to enjoy highly sublime feelings and sentiments. Through that mind we begin to discover what is really meant by universal love and nonviolence. That mind becomes truly healthy and serves as a source of immense inspiration for ourselves and others.

Master of Circumstances

When we acquire a mind such as that, a mind permeated by the blessed meekness referred to by Lord Jesus, we "inherit the earth." We become the master of all the circumstances, conditions, and developments within the material world around us. None of these can pressure our mind any longer. Like a lotus, we bloom above all the conditions of the lake of the world, and remain untouched by them. Like a swan, we sport in the lake of the world, but at any moment we can shake our wings, throw off all the water particles, and fly away.

Thus, when true meekness arises, we attain dominion over the material world. The world of matter does not matter anymore. In Vedantic terminology, we triumph over *māyā* or cosmic illusion, and are no longer tempted by worldly values.

The abundance of the earth is for the desireless, not for the person with desires. When a person approaches the objects of the world with desire, he becomes a slave to them. The objects begin to overpower him and it becomes impossible for him to possess them in the true sense. Desires create slavery to the objects of the world and a slavish mentality degrades the soul.

But in the state of true meekness, the soul submits itself to God alone. It is not tied to the objects through the strings of desires. Therefore, it recovers its mastery over the earth. It rules matter; it commands circumstances; and it acquires a supreme victory that echoes with an immeasurable sense of inner triumph.

Speaking of the qualities of a saint, the great Indian Saint Chaitanya, sang: "He who is humbler than a blade of grass, and yet, more enduring than a tree; he who gives respect to those who lack it—he is ever immersed in singing the praises of the Lord at all times."

These words describe the characteristics of great men and women, people whose spiritual majesty endows them with utter humility and powerful endurance just as blades of grass bend willingly and without complaint beneath the feet of those who walk upon them, a person of true meekness submits himself joyfully to the unfoldment of the Divine Will. Just as a mango tree gives its sweet fruit to a child who throws stones at its branches, or a sandalwood tree gives its exquisite fragrance to the very ax with which it was struck, a man of true meekness radiates a spontaneous tolerance and endurance under all circumstances.

A person of true humility ever delights in making other people feel happy and content. Because of the spiritual strength that flows from within his heart, he does not try to seek any consolation or praise for himself. Rather, he spontaneously showers others with honor, support, and encouragement.

One who has reached great spiritual heights experiences such an overpowering sense of internal expansion that ego spontaneously loses all its importance. His mind then flows spontaneously to God at all times. There is another saying in Sanskrit: "*Namanti phalino vṛkṣaḥ.*" "A tree that is laden with fruit bows down." The implication of this saying is that when prosperity comes to us, when we are endowed with the blessings of life, humility should develop. If prosperity makes one conceited, that prosperity is unhealthy prosperity, envenomed prosperity—like tasty food which has deadly poison in it.

One who is truly humble and prosperous becomes a flawless instrument in Divine Hands, without ever thinking to take the credit for the miraculous results achieved by the Cosmic Will working through him. "How great is this work that I have done!" is never asserted by one who has attained the blessed state of meekness or humility. In the overflowing sense of fulfillment that accompanies his mental expansion, he knows that it is not the ego, but the Divine Will that works through human beings, producing great wonders.

XI

The Egoless Attitude

By Swami Chinmayananda

When we try to form a picture of an egoless person we tend to think of someone who is without any personality, ambition, or assertiveness. It appears to be a life of impotent sleepwalking without any dynamism. A generation of such individuals would be ineffectual in action and dangerous for the community. It would certainly not be conducive for worldly progress, or happy communal living. This may be the impression that we will be left with when we try to grasp the attitude of an egoless person in the community. But if this was so, Lord Krishna would not have advised Arjuna to maintain this psychological mood in the midst of the Mahabharata war. In fact, in Chapter V of the *Bhagavad Gītā*, verses 5-12, Lord Krishna explains this egoless attitude in such a direct and subjective style that any sincere student can easily come to understand this state.

Ego is the sense of "doership" that we bring into all our actions. This "I-do" mentality asserts our individual responsibility for bringing about certain inner and outer conditions in the world and in our relationships with people. Thereafter, the ego unnecessarily carries a heavy load of meaningless and empty responsibilities.

A river moves; it moves by its own nature. If we were to sit on a rock and paddle our feet in the water, it would be for the sheer joy of it. But to feel, and then assert that our paddling is the cause for the entire river movement that is the play of the ego. The anxiety and strain which we then experience from trying to maintain the flow of the river are the hollow rewards of this false attitude. If we sit in a train, we need not push the train and declare that we are making the train move. Therefore, let us live and serve as best as we can, without ego, and egocentric desires. Only then can our lives become an inspiration—a joyous march to success, with overflowing peace, cheer, and goodwill.

Ordinarily we act with ego, and such selfish actions bring psychological bondage, provided by the *vāsanā-s* (mental impressions), which are produced during our actions. Lord Krishna's thesis is that we can bring about a release from our present psychological encumbrances through our actions. The question is how? What adjustments and subtle training are necessary so that each of us can, by living in the right way, earn this inner freedom?

The Lord exhaustively enumerates:

> With an intellect purified by dedicated actions, mind conquered, and senses subdued, one who realizes his Self as the Self in all beings, though acting, is not tainted. (*Gītā* V:7)

By pursuing our daily duties in a spirit of selfless dedication, the *vāsanā-s* exhaust themselves and consequently the intellect becomes purified of its disturbing eruptions of desire. When the intellect becomes quiet, the mind automatically becomes calmer. Once the mind has discovered a climate of joyous peace, the sense organs become subdued and they no longer rush out for their gratifications. Thus, a holy sense of well being, and an unearthly contentment come to dance in the heart of such an individual, as he discovers a new kingdom of meaningful happiness in himself—the state of Selfhood.

Once the ego-precipitating, body, mind, and intellect identifications have ended, the seeker discovers the glorious truth;

that the Self in him is the Self of all. The entire world now stands, without its bewildering clamor of names and forms, and likes and dislikes completely bare, as the Self-of-all. This is a different plane of Consciousness altogether, and therefore the actions in the familiar planes of waking, dream, and sleep no longer affect him. When one has awakened from a dream, the dreamer's actions no longer affect the waker. In the same way, one who has awakened to the higher Consciousness can no longer be affected by his actions in the lower planes. He no longer has the "I-do" mentality, as the sense of being a separate individuality—the ego—has been sublimated upon his new enlightenment.

When a sage thus acts in this consciousness of universality and supreme divinity, what exactly will be his attitude in life?

'I do nothing at all,' thus would the harmonized knower of Truth think, as he is seeing, hearing, touching, smelling, eating, moving, sleeping, breathing, speaking, letting go, seizing, opening, and closing the eyes, convinced that the senses move among the sense objects. (*Gītā* V:8,9)

The one who has realized this essential Truth, centered in the Self, comes to think, "I do nothing at all." He hears, sees, touches, smells, eats, sleeps, breathes, and speaks, but in none of these physical activities has he any sense of "doership." From this state of inner awareness he watches and experiences that "it is the senses that move among the sense objects."

In this new state of Self he is able to watch his own body functioning among the sense objects. He becomes a mere "witness" even to his own physical responses and mental reactions to the world around him. And just as the destiny of our own shadow never affects us, the egoless person, when awakened to the higher plane, comes to feel such a complete detachment from his own physical, mental, and intellectual personalities that he is able to be a creative observer of himself at all times. It is during such egoless moments that the higher abilities flood through us, and we serve the world in divine inspiration.

Throughout such activities there is an enchanting divine glow, a serene godly meaning, and an unearthly grace.

Intelligent Detachment

Thus, the egoless person is a dynamic servant of the community, undertaking all activities with an extra dash and a divine purpose. His performance always has the added charm of inspired efficiency, and the brilliance of a perfect act masterly executed.

It is the selfish ego in us that chains our abilities and hampers our performance. To release ourselves from our limited ego is to explode into a larger realm of a divine personality. The attitude of egolessness is the secret of unveiling the nobler and the dynamic in us, thereby easily crossing over our own imperfections and walking into an ampler field of beauty in all works of life.

When we are in deep-sleep, or under chloroform, we are unconscious and, at such moments, we experience a total absence of ego. From this experience, which is common to all, we are tempted to feel that the egoless state is a state of utter negation— a state of zero action, with no awareness of anything. But Lord Krishna considers an egoless attitude to be the most productive in the dynamic field of action. Therefore, the state of egolessness mentioned in the scriptures cannot be the negative state of "absence of ego," or "absence of consciousness of things within and without."

In the previous verses the Lord explained to us the attitude of egolessness, being a complete elimination of the "I-do" mentality in all our physical and mental functions. Such a total cessation of "doership" is possible only when we transcend into the higher plane of Consciousness. The dreamer, when awakened, can renounce his "doership" in the happenings of the dream. Similarly, the sense of "doership" cannot disappear completely until our ego-consciousness awakens to the Self—

the *Brahmic* Consciousness. The way and the goal are one—by surrendering the ego we strive to "awake" to the Higher—and when fully awakened to the Higher, the ego gets totally surrendered. Therefore the Lord said,

> He who does actions, forsaking attachments, offering them to *Brahman*, abandoning attachment, is not tainted by sin, just as a lotus leaf remains unaffected by the water on it. (*Gītā* V:10)

In this verse we have a prescription by which every one of us can come to live the life of intelligent detachment in life. The way in which we train ourselves to renounce the sense of agency will be a problem for all true students of the *Gītā,* who want to *live* the *Gītā* and not just talk about its ideas. Total detachment is impossible for the human mind, and that is exactly what spiritual seekers often fail to understand. As long as there is a mind, it has to attach itself to something. Therefore, detachment from the false can be successful only when we attach ourselves to the Real.

This psychological fact is scientifically brought out in this verse, wherein Lord Krishna advises all seekers to surrender their attachments to *Brahman* and continue to strive. To remember an ideal constantly, is to become more and more attuned to the perfections of the ideal. In order that we may surrender all our sense of agency for our actions to *Brahman,* we have to remember this concept of Truth as often as we now remember our limited ego. When the frequency of our thoughts upon the Lord becomes as high as the frequency with which we now remember the ego-idea, we shall come to realize the *Brahman*-ideal as intimately as we now know our own ego. In short, today we are "Ego-Realized Souls," and the *Gītā's* call to us is to become "Soul-Realized Egos."

Once our Real Nature is realized, the actions of the body, mind, and intellect can no more leave any impression upon the Self. Merits and demerits belong to the ego and never to the

Ātman. The imperfections of our reflections in a mirror can only be because of the distortions in the reflecting surface. The reflections may look short or long according to the type of mirror into which we are looking. Similarly, the ego comes to suffer the perfect and the imperfect reactions of its own actions.

Having thus realized the Self, to remain in the envelopments of matter and their world of objects, is to remain ever perfectly detached "as the lotus leaf in the water." Even though the lotus leaf exists only in water, draws its nourishment from it and dies in the same water, yet, during its life as a leaf, it does not allow itself to be moistened by water. Similarly, a saint in the world, as a matter-entity, draws nourishment for his individual existence from the world of objects but remains perfectly detached from his own merits and demerits, from his own concepts of beauty and ugliness, and from his own likes and dislikes in the world.

Here we have a technique of renouncing our sense of agency in our actions described exhaustively, which is the method by which ordinary karma can be transformed into *karma yoga.*

This is no strange theory; nor is it a unique doctrine. At every moment, all around the world, we see this happen in many ways. A doctor's attachment to his wife makes him incapable of performing an operation on her, although the same doctor may perform the same operation upon another patient, towards whom he has no self-deluding attachment. If we were to act as representatives of the Infinite, we would discover greater effectiveness and possibilities within ourselves, which are all wasted today by our misconceptions of being a finite ego.

How does a person work with such an egoless attitude? Will not the newly generated *vāsanā-s* shackle his personality with newly forged chains? No. Can he come to liberate himself through work? Yes, as Lord Krishna points out in the following verse:

Yogis, having abandoned attachment, perform actions merely by the body, mind, intellect and senses, for the purification of the self (ego). (*Gītā* 5:11)

Those who perform all their actions in a Yagna-spirit, with total dedication, are called *karma yogin-s*. They merely allow their mind, intellect, and organs of actions-and-perceptions to act as a service of the Lord, without getting themselves selfishly involved in the actions and their fruits. *Karma yogin-s* serve the world for their own individual inner purification.

The ego and egocentric desires together constitute "attachment." This term "attachment" is used quite often in the *Gītā* and everywhere it indicates our ego and egocentric desires that come to play in all our activities. Renouncing this pair within when we act, the existing *vāsanā-s* exhaust themselves, and our mind and intellect become calm, peaceful, steady. This psychological state of meditative poise within is called "purity of heart."

The person who has successfully subdued his entire outgoing personality realizes, in his inward meditation, that as the Self, he is pure Consciousness, in whose presence the equipments get propelled to actions. With such an egoless attitude, the noblest of activities gush out from the inspired saint. It is from those actions, flooding from such a depersonalized one, that the worlds of spirituality, science, politics, and economics gained their growth and development. We all owe today's progress in science and culture, law and order, inventions and discoveries to people working in this egoless attitude of inspiration with a touch of divine creativity. It is through such egoless action that everyone can help remake the floundering world around them.

XII

Abandonment to His Divine Will

by Jean-Pierre de Caussade

If we have abandoned ourselves, there is only one rule for us: the duty of the present moment. The soul is as light as a feather, as fluid as water, as simple as a child, and as lively as a ball in responding to all the impulses of grace. We are like molten metal which takes the shape of the mold into which it is poured, and can just as easily assume any form God wishes to give us. We are like the air which stirs continually, or water which fills every vessel no matter what its shape.

We must offer ourselves to God like a clean, smooth canvas and not worry ourselves about what God may choose to paint on it, for we have perfect trust in Him, have abandoned ourselves to Him, and are so busy doing our duty that we forget ourselves and all our needs. The more closely we devote ourselves to our little task, which is so simple, so secret, and so hidden and apparently so paltry, the more does God enrich and adorn it: "God works wonders for those He loves." (*Psalms* 4:3)

The Master Sculptor

It is true that a canvas simply and blindly offered to the brush feels at each moment only the stroke of the brush. It is the same with a lump of stone. Each blow from the hammering of the sculptor's chisel makes it feel, if it could, as if it were being destroyed. As blow after blow descends, the stone knows nothing of how the sculptor is shaping it. All it feels is a chisel chopping away at it, cutting it and mutilating it.

For example, let's take a piece of stone destined to be carved into a crucifix or a statue. We might ask it: "What do you think is happening to you?" And it might answer: "Don't ask me. All I know is that I must stay immovable in the hands of the sculptor, and I must love him and endure all he inflicts on me to produce the figure he has in mind. He knows how to do it. As for me, I have no idea what he is doing, nor do I know what he will make of me. But what I do know is that his work is the best possible. It is perfect. I welcome each blow of his chisel as the best thing that could happen to me, although, if I'm to be truthful, I feel that every one of these blows is ruining me, destroying me and dis-figuring me. But I remain unconcerned. I concentrate on the present moment, think only of my duty, and suffer all that this master sculptor inflicts on me without knowing his purpose or fretting about it."

Yes, leave to God what is His business, and carry on peace-fully with your work. Be quite sure that whatever happens to your spiritual life or to your activities in the world is always for the best. Let God act, and abandon yourself to Him. Let the chisel and the brush do their work, even though the brush covers the canvas with so many colors that, instead of a picture, it seems there is only a daub. Let us work together with the will of God by a steady and simple submission, a complete forgetful-ness of self, and concentration on our duties. Let us go straight ahead. Never mind the lack of a map, ignore the lie of the land, and take no notice of the places you pass through. Keep going and you will attain all you desire. Everything will be given to you, if with love and obedience you seek God's kingdom and His righteousness.

XIII

Self-Surrender

Edited by Madan Mohan Varma

[*The following article is taken from the book* A Saint's Call to Mankind. *In this book Madan Mohan Varma brought together discourses by a saint who prefers to remain anonymous.*]

Self-surrender is the key to God-realization: it is the strength of the weak, the life of the *sādhaka* (spiritual seeker), the final effort and the trump-card of the devotee, the sheet anchor of the theist, the unfailing medicine for the sorrow-stricken, and the prayer of the fallen. Self-surrender gives strength to the weak, vouchsafes *siddhi-s* (spiritual powers) to the *sādhaka*, the Beloved to the lover, God to His devotee, happiness to the server, holiness to the sinner, freedom to the bound one, immortality to mortal man.

Every man surrenders himself to someone. The only difference is that the theist surrenders to the One and the materialist surrenders himself to many; the former fulfils his real want and the latter runs after innumerable shadows of desires. Real want once fulfilled ceases to be, whereas desires arise again and again.

Self-surrender is an attitude of mind, which exalts the "I" of the devotee. It is not any particular form of action. Nor is the feeling "I am His" a matter of practice. It is a *bhāva* (feeling). Once it is enthroned in the heart, it sprouts forth into all such *sādhanā* (spiritual practices) or actions as necessary, even as a seed once sown sprouts into a tree in due course. Prior to self-surrender the 'I' of a person remains a bundle of desires. Self-surrender dissolves all desires into one desire. Then the person who has surrendered himself to God may seem to others to be performing many actions; but they are only like the acting on a stage for the benefit of the world. His inner life is one-pointed.

No one is too low to be accepted by the Lord. No mother, even in our world, denies her unclean child her love. Surely if we rush into the Lord's bosom as His children, He will not refuse to own us. The greatest mistake we commit is that, on the path to the Lord, we create so many hillocks of desire on which we pause to rest, even though if we have once surrendered ourselves, the Lord comes more than half-way to blast those hurdles with His Grace. The Grace of the Lord is not less than the might of the Ganges which washes off all the dirt in its way.

If you surrender yourself wholly and completely to the Lord, you need not even worry about your progress on the path. Have complete faith in the Lord. The wise gardener, once he has sown his seeds, has faith in their growth, and does not dig in every day to observe their growth. Thereby he would only make their growth impossible.

The devotee who has surrendered to God looks to no one except to his Lord for the fulfilment of his own wants though he fulfils the wants of others, acting for a while as an ideal friend, an ideal son, an ideal father, an ideal husband, an ideal wife, an ideal unit of society, and so on.

All virtues are manifested in the devotee who has surrendered himself to the Lord without effort, and all his vices vanish: because all vices arise from egoism and all virtues from egolessness and, the devotee having surrendered his ego to the Lord, the Lord dissolves his ego.

It is amazing that we run after the world which constantly spurns us, and turn our back upon the Lord who is ever ready to take us unto His bosom.

The individual who is conscious of his virtues and his

capacity for *sādhanā* obtains divine grace after exhausting his consciousness of the same; whereas the devotee who finds himself utterly powerless or unworthy of doing anything of his own is drawn close to God by God's own grace. Dependence on God's grace is the most unfailing sheet anchor of the devotee.

Let the devotee tell all his organs of action and senses of perception, as well as the mind, "I am going to meet my Beloved. By your good offices I have gained full experience of the shadowy nature of the world and have done with it! You please rest now."

"I cannot exist without You;" this call of the devotee makes him entitled to meet God. Such a devotee cannot spare any thought for the past, nor indulge in any hopes for the future; he is only restless in his yearning in the present.

It is only when one exhausts one's sense of gratification from the consciousness of one's service to fellow-beings, activities, fame, and so on, that one is able to surrender oneself to God. Until one is able to surrender oneself, one should constantly and earnestly pray to God to give him the capacity for complete surrender. After turning his face to God and becoming entirely His, there are no more obligations for the devotee to discharge. By right action all propensity for egoistic action dies by itself.

Intense Yearning

Remembrance of God, concentration, and meditation are not equivalent to the fullness of love, and a real devotee should not be content with them. Let the devotee who begs for favors beg for the Bestower of favors Himself, so that he would not have to beg again and again.

Intense yearning to meet Him and restlessness without Him is a self-sufficient and final *sādhanā* for the devotee. Just as the dawn of the sun scatters all darkness, so the awakening of deep yearning for the Godhead burns away all of one's egoism, which is the root of all vices.

Just as a mother feeds her child only to the measure of its hunger, so does the Divine Mother feed us to the measure of our hunger. She, however, by Her divine dispensation, goes on ending our temporary pleasures, to teach us renunciation of fleeting pleasures in favor of happiness eternal.

"I am His" is the *mahā-mantra* for the devotee, which resolves or dissolves all his problems by God's omnipotent grace.

We are like thirsty souls floating on infinite waters. If only we turn our face to God, our thirst will be quenched, and quenched for all time.

Even as fire turns all wood put into it into flames, so does God turn the most sinful of men, who become His, into His infinite beatitude. For one grain of devotion offered to Him, He showers tons and tons of His Love. He who realizes this ineffable greatness of God will but melt in gratitude!

Let not the *sādhakā* think that he cannot realize God because he lacks this or that quality or virtue. God cannot be purchased by any quality or virtue that there may be in mortal man. *Sādhanā* is not the price of His compassion. *Sādhanā* is meant only to rid us of our forgetfulness in regard to God, and to awaken in us the sole aspiration to return to Him. Such aspiration is not in the least dependent on any paraphernalia, possessions, qualities, or circumstances. It is only a kindling of the feeling of kinship with God, which can take place in all circumstance. In fact, all esoteric *sādhanā-s* to spiritualize our lives are like irrigating the fields with waters drawn from the well; whereas to let the Divine pour into our being is like the clouds drawing water from the sea and pouring it back upon the fields to irrigate them.

Just as a faithful wife performs all actions with the sole object of pleasing her husband, and serves her husband, his relatives, and his friends to please him. So does the devotee perform all actions for the sake of his Lord and to please his Lord by serving His creatures. Just as a faithful wife serves her husband for the joy of serving him, but is nevertheless looked after by her husband in all respects, so the devotee, while wanting nothing for himself except God's pleasure, is looked after by God—who is infinitely more resourceful than the earthly husband—in all respects. Or, even as one who goes into a garden to buy fruits obtains shade and pure air automatically, so the devotee has all his wants fulfilled when he turns his face to the Divine.

Those who approach God for the fulfilment of any personal desires often turn away from Him after the fulfilment of desires. True love of God is not for what God could give or gives, but for Himself.

Whatever things—including one's mind and body—are dedicated to God become purified and turn into tools of worship.

Pleasure, pain, fear, anxiety, and so on, hold no sway over the devotee. The feeling of kinship with God—to feel as a veritable child of God—is the most direct approach to Him. To make the best and most righteous use of one's environment is the best outer *sādhanā* for the devotee. To distribute the pleasures which come to him in the service of others, and to learn the lesson of renunciation from all the pain that comes, are the spontaneous characteristics of his conduct.

The devotee is only a soldier of God. Even a mountain-like piece of work is not a strain on him when it is the will of God that he should do it. The devotee has no power of his own; but the source of his power is the unlimited power of God Himself when He wills to do a thing through him.

The devotee regards his every activity as an instrument of worship. Therefore, in his inner mind there is no difference between one activity and another, between a small piece of work and a big work, between one aspect of activity and another. For him, all work becomes worship; for all his work is "unto God," a part played by him on His stage for His pleasure.

God, indeed, yearns for the devotee who yearns for Him! But such a devotee is utterly indifferent to all else; even in suffering he rejoices in his Lord's will for him. Most people, however, think of God or pray to Him for some desired objects, or for pleasant circumstances, not for Him.

As water is drawn up to the source when its flow is plugged, so is man drawn up to the Divine when he withdraws himself from the objects of the senses and stands *alone*, naked, renouncing his body and mind and their relationships—the spark returning to the Flame, the individual (*jīva*) returning to the bosom of his Father.

One-pointedness is the essence of devotion. Just as to the seeker of sense objects his religious performances are tantamount to self-seeking and self-indulgence, so to the aspirant for God all his spontaneous works become modes of worship.

There may be said to be five stages on the path of devotion. First, acceptance; second, faith; third, relationship, that is, the forging of the 'link'; fourth, constant remembrance; and the fifth, love or unbroken *bhakti*, which is the fruit of self-surrender.

As we realize the oceanic greatness, grace, and compassion of God, all desire for sense objects melts away, and the child of man is reborn as the Child of God. The "twice-born child" is drawn close to God by the very ecstasy of his newly discovered *kinship* with his Father. The need for outer *sādhanā-s* is then exhausted for him; the panorama is found changed; a silent 'revolution' has taken place; he seeks no more favors of God, but only delights in *total* surrender to the Lord of Love, infinite and ineffable.

Self-surrender, therefore, is the ultimate *sādhanā* on the path of devotion; there is nothing else to do for one who catches a glimpse of the infinite ocean of God's grace and His unbounded compassion. It is a heavenly nectar which comes to those who have dissolved all self-consciousness and pride, and whose desires have all fused into the single desire of meeting the Beloved. Such a devotee does not have to wait for God, but God awaits him.

Pronunciation of Sanskrit Letters

a	(b*u*t)	k	(*s*kate)	t	⎰ *th*ink or	ś	(*sh*ove)
ā	(f*a*ther)	kh	(*K*ate)	th	⎱ *th*ird	ṣ	(bu*sh*el)
i	(*i*t)	g	(*g*ate)	d	⎰ *th*is or	s	(*s*o)
ī	(b*ee*t)	gh	(*g*awk)	dh	⎱ *th*ere	h	(*h*um)
u	(s*u*ture)	ṅ	(*s*ing)	n	(*n*umb)	ṁ	(nasaliza-
ū	(p*oo*l)	c	(*ch*unk)	p	(s*p*in)		tion of
ṛ	(*r*ig)	ch	(mat*ch*)	ph	(loo*ph*ole)		preceding
ṝ	(*rrr*ig)	j	(*J*ohn)	b	(bu*n*)		vowel)
ḷ	⎰ no	jh	(*j*am)	bh	(ru*b*)	ḥ	(aspira-
	⎪ English	ñ	(bu*n*ch)	m	(*m*uch)		tion of
	⎨ equiva-	ṭ	(*t*ell)	y	(*y*oung)		preceding
	⎩ lent	ṭh	(*t*ime)	r	(d*r*ama)		vowel)
e	(pl*ay*)	ḍ	(*d*uck)	l	(*l*uck)		
ai	(h*i*gh)	ḍh	(*d*umb)	v	(*w*ile/*v*ile)		
o	(t*o*e)	ṇ	(u*n*der)				
au	(c*o*w)						

For information contact:
Chinmaya Mission West Publications Division
Distribution Office
560 Bridgetown Pike
Langhorne, PA 19053, USA
Phone: (215) 396-0390   Fax: (215) 396-9710
Toll Free: 1-888-CMW-READ (1-888-269-7323)

The Sanskrit word *Mananam* means reflection. The *Mananam* series of books is dedicated to the exposition of Vedantic thought, with an emphasis on the unity of all religions. It is published by Chinmaya Mission West, which was founded by Swami Chinmayananda in 1975. Swami Chinmayananda pursued the spiritual path in the Himalayas, under the guidance of Swami Sivananda and Swami Tapovanam. He is credited with the awakening of India and the rest of the world to the ageless wisdom of Vedanta. He taught the logic of spirituality and emphasized that selfless work, study, and meditation are the cornerstones of spiritual practice. His legacy remains in the form of books, audio and video tapes, schools, social service projects, and Vedanta teachers whom he taught and inspired and now serve their local communities all around the world.